THE CENTRE FOR ENVIRONMENTAL STUDIES SERIES
General Editor: David Donnison

THE ORGANIZATION OF HOUSING

This book is one of a series edited at the
Centre for Environmental Studies and published
on its behalf by Heinemann Educational Books
Ltd. The series will present work in the fields
of planning, and urban and regional studies.
The Centre is an independent research
foundation charged with the furtherance and
dissemination of research in these fields. Further
information about this series and the Centre's
work can be obtained from the General Editor.

The Organization of Housing

*Public and Private Enterprise
in London*

MICHAEL HARLOE
RUTH ISSACHAROFF
RICHARD MINNS

Foreword by
PROFESSOR R. E. PAHL

 Heinemann : London

Heinemann Educational Books Ltd

London Edinburgh Melbourne Auckland Toronto
Hong Kong Singapore Kuala Lumpur
Ibadan Nairobi Johannesburg
Lusaka New Delhi

ISBN 0 435 85923 4
© Centre for Environmental Studies 1974
First published 1974

Published by Heinemann Educational Books Ltd
48 Charles Street, London W1X 8AH

Printed in Great Britain by
Richard Clay (The Chaucer Press), Ltd,
Bungay, Suffolk

Contents

Foreword
by Professor R. E. Pahl

It is a sad but inescapable fact that despite considerable academic research and political intervention, the housing situation in the capital of one of the richest nations in the world is still a cause for serious concern. Homelessness is increasing and the rate of physical obsolescence is likely to increase in the late 1970s and early 1980s. There is a strong likelihood according to the GLC Housing Survey,[1] that in ten years from now the physical condition of the housing stock will be worse than it is today.

Now that it is recognized that national figures of habitable dwellings in relation to potential households bear little relation to specific housing problems in specific areas, there has been a tendency to assume that there is simply a residual problem left in certain specific unfortunate areas. Focusing extra resources in these areas has not, however, produced noticeably positive results. Neither the tools of the Right—enterprise, private initiative, and market mechanisms—nor the tools of the Left— public responsibility and public controls—have provided *the* answer. Indeed, as housing policy has lurched from one piece of legislation to the next so the unintended consequences of each have remained in a complex and compounded form so that a wide range of powers are available to public and private agencies together with a wide range of possible means of preventing or delaying the use of these powers.

Anyone turning to this book for clear and unequivocal answers to the dilemmas that have faced successive Ministers of Housing is likely to be disappointed; in my view this is the

---

[1] Greater London Council (1970). *The Condition of London's Housing—A Survey* (GLC Department of Planning and Transportation Research Report No. 4, August 1970).

great merit of the three authors' work. Associated with the problem of the use and distribution of the surplus generated by productive work is the problem of providing decent housing of the right size, in the right place, at a price the people can afford. That these two problems cannot be considered separately and in isolation is becoming increasingly clear. This point was already grasped by the Chairman of the LCC's Housing of the Working Classes Committee, who wrote towards the end of the nineteenth century: 'The Housing problem indeed may be said to be the sum and total of all the social and economic problems which await solution,' for, he felt that at bottom, 'it provokes the vexed question of the relation between rent and wages, which easily slides into that of capital and labour.'[2]

It would be very surprising if a Minister of Housing could easily solve that kind of 'vexed question'. Yet so much research, both within government departments and outside, assumes that this or that cluster of piecemeal reforms will 'solve' the housing problem. The expansion of both public and private ownership carries a specific set of problems—the former involving questions of management and allocation and the latter problems of finance and credit. It is just not easy organizing a balance between public and private interests, which are very often in conflict with one another.

Inevitably, then, a study of the organization of housing must raise fundamental questions about the control and the allocation of economic surpluses and about the basic weaknesses of a mixed economy. There are those who would argue that endemic homelessness and a residual housing problem is a price we as a society must be prepared to pay for the benefits of a system which controls excesses of private greed and of public bureaucratization. Certainly apologists for both conservative and radical ideologies are given awkward questions to answer by the analysis presented in this book. It is perhaps a weakness in presentation that the authors have not emphasized, as much as they might, the full significance of their work. It is clear that all organizations have constraints within themselves and from the external environment in which they operate. Those who devise

---

[2] See A. S. WOHL, 'The Housing of the Working Classes in London 1815–1914' in *The History of Working Class Housing*, S. D. Chapman (editor) (Newton Abbot: 1971).

policies which must operate either nationally or locally must assume that an organizational form can be devised which will work the way it is supposed to do. Even the authors of this book show only a rudimentary understanding of organizational theory and analysis. Government is based on the positivistic assumption that one can gather the appropriate 'facts', which, after subjection to rational and logical intelligence, can provide the basis for the solution of specific problems by specific policies. That the organization may not be able to implement the rational solutions thus proposed, or that organizations may be in conflict with each other or within themselves, reflecting broader conflicts over the use of economic surpluses generally, is forgotten. The whole ideology of 'the Welfare State' with its technologists—the social administrators—and its technicians— the planners, housing managers, social workers, and so forth— is based on an implied social consensus and the belief in the ultimate capacity of organizations to adapt most efficiently to the tasks set them.

This book adds the further complexities of differential needs, their determination in different areas, and other aspects consequent upon geographic location. This raises the question of how far local autonomy is necessary for the determination of specific policies geared to local circumstances and how far local interests need to be overruled in order to meet national priorities.

Inevitably, then, the government and organization of housing involves clashes between ideologies and values. The Church of England is obliged to manage its property more efficiently in terms of higher rental income at the expense of equity. The Conservative Party in Lambeth was obliged to use strong powers of public control in the interests of the efficient use of its housing stock. The activities of Shelter and other worthy voluntary associations had to be curtailed, since they were getting in each other's way. This study demonstrates over and over again how policies and organizations can get at cross purposes with one another. The basic constraints which the various organizations faced are clearly and cogently outlined and some of these can be overcome through piecemeal reforms and interventions.

The authors argue for an end to compromise. Assuming parity between different agencies and organizations is itself a bias. What is needed is a positive bias in the direction of greatest need, by the agency most likely to achieve the best results.

To a large extent Britain has got a more humane and generous approach to housing than other, ostensibly richer, societies. This is largely due to the size and quality of its local authority housing, which despite what its critics would say, is probably the best-managed, publicly-owned housing stock in the world. It is an enormous asset to our society and should not lightly be allowed to diminish.

Yet curiously local authority housing lacks its champions: our educational system and the National Health Service have their respective supporters and admirers but 'council housing' has become more an indication of 'problems', 'trouble' or poverty. In rural areas the council estates are simply not seen or acknowledged by the property owners and in towns, as Peter Collison's classic study *The Cuttesloe Walls* describes, the division between the council estate and private housing can be a source of sharp social conflict.

By allowing our best housing asset to acquire this social stigma we have handicapped ourselves enormously. Yet, curiously, the Labour Party did not seem to grasp this during the 1960s and followed what they presumably saw as an electorally more appealing policy in supporting the move towards increasing home ownership. Both parties disapproved of the private landlord—the Labour Party because landlordism carried with it notions of rapacious profit and the Conservative Party because some extra greedy and unscrupulous landlords were bringing the system based on the pursuit of private gain and profit into disrepute. The increasing housing problem of our capital city during the 1960s was an embarrassment to both parties as the legislation passed to clear up the unintended consequences of the previous legislation led in turn to its own crop of unintended consequences.

It is clear that the authors of this study have been led by their analysis to feel that the present 'amalgam of directive and per-missive powers controlled by various, often conflicting, pro-cesses of accountability' is unsatisfactory and that for them, tinkering with a system, the complexities of which are not fully understood, is unlikely to be of much help. Yet they do not feel that any sweeping new change will be an automatic panacea.

Unlike many of those who have concerned themselves with the practical problems of housing they see the difficulties in both piecemeal ameliorism *and* more radical 'clean sweep changes' involving new bureaucratic and administrative systems. The strong powers of the state in countries like Hungary and Czechoslovakia do not necessarily seem able to handle the complex problems of social justice which the allocation procedures of housing must imply.

The authors are in danger of being attacked by everyone: the policy-oriented social administrator will deplore the lack of positive, pragmatic proposals for reform; the radicals will scorn the poverty of academicism; and the academics will wish that the most important implications for our understanding of 'the welfare state' as a type of society had been more fully explored. Yet the authors should be congratulated on the success they have achieved in describing the ambiguities of reality. This book has a lasting value for its descriptive analysis. Others may build on this both practically and theoretically. Glib generalizations and simple-minded political proposals will be much less easy to make by those who have read this book. I take this to be a clear advance: *The Organization of Housing* is a step forward in our understanding. If that does not necessarily make the 'answers' immediately easier to find, it should at least ensure that they are better ones in the end.

Canterbury, October 1973

Preface

The research which is reported on in this book was carried out in 1969–72 with aid of a grant from the Social Science Research Council. The grant was originally awarded to Professor David Donnison and Dr Peter Levin at the London School of Economics in 1967 to investigate aspects of the development of new and expanding towns. Subsequently an extension of the scope of the grant to cover the organization of housing in London was agreed and the authors of the book became principally responsible for this section of the work. Dr Levin remained responsible for the work on new and expanding towns and his work is being published separately.

Many people and organizations have given us material and intellectual help. We can only acknowledge here our debts to those on whom we imposed the greatest burdens. The Centre for Environmental Studies provided an ideal base from which to work. Despite the fact that we were officially members of the LSE staff, the Centre made available to us all the facilities it offers to its own staff. David Donnison, in this dual role as Director of the Centre and principal recipient of our grant, did all he could to ensure that the administration of our project ran smoothly. In addition he patiently sat through dozens of meetings with us during the course of the project in which our ideas and progress were systematically, and sometimes painfully, reviewed. We very much appreciate the help he gave us.

Working at the Centre for Environmental Studies brought us into contact with a wide range of people involved in urban research who were working, visiting, or connected with CES in some way. We benefited from many of these exchanges. In particular however Martin Rein, Oliver P. Williams, and Ray Pahl exercised a crucial influence on our thinking at different stages of the project and David Eversley and Peter Levin both helped us to define our research in its early stages.

Our greatest debt of gratitude must be however to the large number of individuals who gave us help in the areas and agencies we investigated. Virtually all our questions and requests for information were met willingly; something that many people felt some agencies, especially in the private sector of the housing market, would be unwilling to do. This feeling has probably contributed to academics' lack of investigation of the institutional aspects of the housing market in the past. We hope that much more work in this area will now be seen to be possible and worthwhile.

Of all those who provided the raw material for this book we owe particular thanks to the officials and councillors of the Greater London Council and the London Boroughs of Lambeth and Sutton. In many ways their activities form the centre-piece of our study. Consequently our demands on their time and knowledge were high. We think that it would be invidious not to mention two officers by name, Harry Simpson (formerly Director of Housing and Property Services in Lambeth, now Director-General of the Northern Ireland Housing Executive) and Bernard Crofton (formerly Assistant Research and Development Officer in Lambeth, now Senior Administrative Officer of the London Housing Office). Both these officers took a personal interest in our work and went considerably beyond their role as informants in influencing our thinking.

We would also like to thank a long and varied cast of students, friends, and relatives who bore the brunt of the tedious work of data preparation and express special thanks to Juliette London, our secretary throughout much of the project, who must have typed some sections of the manuscript an unimaginable number of times.

The distribution of housing opportunities in our society mirrors the general distribution of life chances—both are grossly unequal. Major changes in the housing situation will require major changes in the wider situation and both require the political will to achieve them. No academic study can contribute directly to mobilizing this will but political demands which are based on an inadequate understanding of the system whose alteration is demanded are apt to be useless, self-defeating, or positively harmful, as the history of many of the more 'radical' social policy interventions demonstrates. We hope that this book will contribute to ensuring that proposals for the radical changes in the distribution of housing opportunities that we would like to see are better founded than hitherto.

January 1974, London M.H. R.I. R.M.

Introduction

Social Policy and Organizations

British social policies are implemented by a diverse range of organizations. These organizations have varying aims and procedures and differing levels of resources. Furthermore they are separately accountable to a wide range of authorities for what they do. These factors constrain organizations and set limits to what they can do.

A study of the diversity of these organizations and their characteristics is important both for social scientists and for policy makers. The academic study of social policy has tended to concentrate on measuring the gaps between the provision of social services on the one hand and individual and group needs on the other. These studies often recommend new or increased levels of service provision within the broad confines of the existing institutional framework. They ignore the organizational reasons for gaps in service provision and they overlook the obstacles to change imposed by this framework.

Similarly policy makers underestimate the diversity of the framework and the constraints on the organizations working within it. This is unfortunate because it gives them a false view of the capabilities of organizations to carry out policies. Policy aims become distorted and crucial areas of individual and group need are ignored.

Housing policy is a good illustration of the limitations in the present approach of academics and policy makers. We now have a great deal of information about gaps in the provision of housing, so much so that David Donnison has called for action from policy makers before any more similar research is conducted [1]. Policy makers for their part have responded to information on housing need by urging organizations to pursue a more 'comprehensive' approach to the provision of housing. The first clear statement of this came from the Labour government, in 1965.

. . . the foundation for a comprehensive national housing plan has now been laid. Governments hitherto have been able to plan forward programmes in the public sector and to have discussions with representatives of the local authorities about financial and other requirements to support those programmes, but it has not been possible to plan house-building as a whole. Now for the first time, the Government, the building societies, and the builders have discussed together and agreed on the need for forward planning of house-building, and for continuous collaboration to ensure a steadily rising programme. For the first time the prerequisites of forward planning, including adequate incentives and flexible controls, are being formulated. It should now be possible, with the new arrangements for regular consultation and review among all the interests concerned, to ensure a steadily rising house-building programme. From this start a comprehensive plan covering all facets of housing policy can be evolved. [2]

The origin and development of the idea of a 'comprehensive' housing policy is closely related to the increasing convergence and consensus between the two major parties in the 1960s over issues of housing policy. The Labour Party had dropped the idea of municipalizing the privately rented sector from its manifesto and become as committed as the Conservatives to promoting owner occupation. Both Labour and Conservative governments accepted the concept of a 'comprehensive' housing policy, an approach which they expected local authorities to adopt. In 1973 the government repeated its exhortations to local authorities, stating that,

A wide view of local authority housing responsibilities is particularly necessary in considering those areas of stress where overcrowding and bad housing are worst. These are the areas where the housing stock is old and in poor condition and where the combination of acute physical and social problems makes action most difficult. . . . Only a comprehensive approach will succeed in curing the ills of these areas. [3]

In this book we shall explain what exactly is implied by the idea of a 'comprehensive' policy, what the limitations are in the idea, what obstacles exist to the implementation of the concept, and finally, what a 'comprehensive' housing policy means in terms of the whole question of the stratification of housing opportunities and its relevance to the spatial pattern of power and access in the city.

London's Housing and the Policy Debate

London is a particularly appropriate area for examining the importance of organizations in the implementation of policy. Within the area of Greater London there is considerable fragmentation of responsibility for the provision of housing, both between the private and the public sectors and among the thirty-three local authorities with housing powers [4].

The information about London's housing need represents a very depressing picture, particularly the inner area, where the majority of problems are concentrated. One detailed statistical report concluded that—

> By far the greatest housing need, therefore, is concentrated in Inner London. A whole range of measures is needed to tackle this problem . . . overspill and planning policies related to employment etc. But these alone cannot solve the problems of Inner London, and London as a whole must help itself as far as it possibly can. This means that the outer parts of London, where there will shortly be a much nearer balance of supply and demand, should do everything possible to help Inner London. If they do not, the result will not merely be that the problems of Inner London will continue to be so much the worse; it could also happen that development in the outer parts would attract a still greater flow of people from outside London, thus making the total problem still more intractable. [5]

Other statistical material showed that despite a continuing drop in the number of households in Inner London[1] the number of dwellings has also been falling as councils build fewer housing units than they knock down. The stock declines in this way mainly because of the competing demands from other services for a limited supply of land—for open space, schools, etc. Some sectors of the housing market have been hit by this decline more than others, especially the privately rented sector—the tenure category in which it is easiest for the worst-off to obtain accommodation. The unfurnished part of that sector, which has the advantage of having its terms of tenancy protected by the 1965 Rent Act, has been declining

---

[1] Here and elsewhere the term Inner London we define as the Group A boroughs used by the GLC in the Greater London Development Plan. See Figure 1, page 7.

most rapidly of all the sectors as a result of local authority demolitions, mainly because of the heavy concentration of older, unfit properties that it contains. It has also fallen as a result of sales to owner occupiers and conversions to furnished lettings which are often more lucrative.

At the same time reports showed that the fall in the number of households has been slowed down by rising headship rates—as households with children leave London, young single people come in so increasing the competition for available space. This has important implications for households with children who are unable to leave and who are unable to improve their housing situation in Inner London itself. The competition for a declining supply of rented accommodation has resulted in multiple occupation which is most acute among tenants and families in furnished accommodation—the most insecure form of tenure. The Francis Committee report [6] found that 78 per cent of the households in furnished accommodation in certain stress areas shared a toilet. Moreover 49 per cent of the households in furnished accommodation in stress areas had children and 14 per cent had three or more children. According to the 1966 Census, sharing was far worse in some boroughs, e.g. Lambeth, Islington, Kensington and Chelsea, than others.

Since the mid-1960s, the comprehensive idea has been interpreted in various ways.

Firstly, some groups have supported a 'co-operative' version of the comprehensive approach. This can involve either actively bargaining with private-sector agencies to get them to meet certain needs, or relying on encouragement and exhortations. The Greater London Council (GLC) for example, has stated that,

> The Council's policy throughout London is that private enter-prise and housing associations should be encouraged to assist the efforts of the public housing authorities. This will increase the choice and variety of housing, give some relief to public financing, and help to create balanced communities. It will reduce the high proportion of owner occupiers in the flows of residents out of London. The Council considers that London housing authorities must bear these advantages in mind and where appropriate should encourage development of housing sites by private developers and housing associations. [7]

Secondly, other authorities have argued that the comprehensive approach should not only involve co-operation and
bargaining with private-sector agencies, but should also
recognize that more positive controls are often necessary.
London boroughs of both party political complexions in
different parts of Greater London accept this 'regulatory' version of a comprehensive policy. It includes, for instance, the
introduction of 'registration' schemes for houses in multiple
occupation.

Thirdly, other policy makers propose that intervention,
failing co-operation, should go even further and include
'municipalization', or actually taking over the privately
rented sector [8], or trying to control conditions in the privately
rented sector by the selective acquisition of properties. It can
also involve pressuring other public agencies to intervene more
in their respective spheres of authority. If, for example, Outer
London should fail to co-operate with Inner London in the
provision of public housing, some people conclude that the
GLC itself should build there, or that inner boroughs should
take some joint action over the contribution that Outer London
might make,[2] or even that a new strategic or metropolitan
housing authority should take over responsibility for London's
overall housing strategy.[3]

The statistical information we have referred to and the range
of policy proposals we have described show two things. Firstly
that there is a division between Inner and Outer London in
terms of housing needs and housing provision. Secondly that
the whole range of public- and private-sector housing agencies
is involved in the policy debate. Our study will therefore take
account of the spatial distribution of housing need and opportunity and the wide range of agencies involved in the differing
proposals outlined above.

---

[2] In 1971 a 'London Housing Office' was proposed by the London
Boroughs Association to, among other things, 'assess help which outer
boroughs might give to inner areas ... and organize people who want to
move'. *The Guardian*, 1 October, 1971.
[3] GLDP, *Report of the Panel of Inquiry* (The Layfield Report) (London:
H.M.S.O., 1973), Vol. 1, p. 193. In order for the basic housing problems
of London to be solved, the Panel suggested that the Minister should
'(a) ... initiate further action on the private rented sector.
  (b) Create a strategic housing authority.'

The Areas and Organizations Chosen

Against the background of the statistics on London's housing needs and the various interpretations of what a 'comprehensive housing policy involves, we set out to discover what the limitations are in the 'comprehensive' approaches by examining the goals and constraints of the organizations concerned and who they are able to house. We will concentrate on the 'comprehensive' approaches adopted by London authorities. These approaches may involve building as many council houses as possible, trying to co-operate with or control the private sector, and relying on whatever public agencies they can to solve some of their problems.

We chose Lambeth in Inner London, Sutton in Outer London, and the GLC because it is the metropolitan authority for the whole of London. We looked at these councils' building programmes, their schemes for lending for house purchase, and their attempts to control or involve the private sector. The private-sector organizations we studied were housing associations, building societies, private developers, private landlords, and estate agents.

Lambeth's housing situation is typical of many of the problems of Inner London we have outlined (see Figure 1). The number of dwellings in the borough has fallen faster than the decline in households, and so sharing of amenities and multiple occupation is common. There are fewer unfit dwellings than normal, but a more than average proportion of dwellings with short 'lives' (dwellings with a life of seven years or less).

In contrast Sutton illustrates the radically different problems and opportunities in Outer London. Here the increase in dwellings has more than kept pace with the increase in households. Sharing and overcrowding are minimal in comparison with Inner London, and unfit and short-life dwellings present no long-term difficulty. There is a far higher degree of owner occupation, a smaller percentage of council dwellings, and significantly less privately-rented property.

All three authorities had different approaches to a 'comprehensive' housing policy—or different housing ideologies.[4]

---

[4] Ideology we define as a belief system about how society—or a significant part of it such as the housing market—does and should operate, about

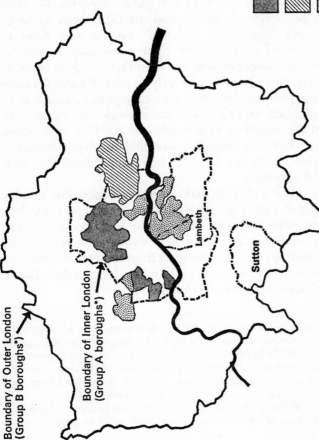

Group A Boroughs*

Camden
City of London
Hackney
Hammersmith
Haringey
Islington
Kensington and
Chelsea

Lambeth
Lewisham
Newham
Southwark
Tower Hamlets
Wandsworth
Westminster

Group B Boroughs*

Barking
Barnet
Bexley
Brent
Bromley
Croydon
Ealing
Enfield
Greenwich
Harrow
Havering

Hillingdon
Hounslow
Kingston upon
Thames
Merton
Redbridge
Richmond upon
Thames
Sutton
Waltham Forest

Residential Areas suffering
from excessive overcrowding
and sharing

Residential Areas in poor
physical condition

Residential Areas suffering
from both the aforementioned
categories

Boundary of Outer London
(Group B boroughs*)

Boundary of Inner London
(Group A boroughs*)

Lambeth

Sutton

(*Source:* Greater London Development Plan. Report of Studies)

Figure I

Sutton and the GLC showed the same basic 'co-operative' ideology but within this broad category there were differences between them. Lambeth adopted a 'regulatory' approach. It differed from the other two authorities in its view of the role of the public sector and it even hoped for help from the GLC and authorities like Sutton. It also differed on why private-sector agencies should be involved in the local housing effort and on what role they should play. All had varying degrees of success.

Apart from differing housing problems these three authorities differ in their approach. In addition one of the comprehensive approaches—that of Lambeth—was partly based on the hope of co-operation with the other two public agencies. We shall therefore be looking at Sutton and the GLC both as 'independent' and 'dependent variables'—on the one hand as housing agencies in their own right attempting to employ comprehensive strategies and on the other hand as agencies being looked to by Lambeth for help as part of *Lambeth*'s comprehensive approach. Sutton is near enough to Lambeth to be able to give help and the GLC has strategic housing powers. We therefore wanted to see not only how the GLC and Sutton went about building council houses and involved themselves with private enterprise, but also how they helped the inner borough of Lambeth.

Thus we deal with four main questions concerning housing policies. Firstly, what are the differences in attitudes, ideology or opportunities between the public and private sector; secondly, what are the differences *within* each sector; and thirdly, what do organizations want from each other, and what success do they have in getting it? Finally, how do these factors vary between different areas of London?

---

how it should distribute resources and 'life chances'. The ideology of the housing association movement, for instance, might be, 'Too much public housing is bad. It limits choice and is subject to impersonal criteria for the assessment of need. The very size of local authorities means that they are out of touch with people's needs. We want far smaller independent agencies which are more sensitive to individual needs.' The value judgement may be backed by evidence but very often judgements are made and concepts used which are not scientifically valid or proven, or even capable of proof.

Conclusion

To summarize this study, our discussion of the organization of housing in London looks at the goals and ideologies of the organizations concerned and the constraints they faced in the implementation of policy.

It is important to emphasize that this study is concerned with both ideologies *and* constraints. Ray Pahl has written that we need to know what effects the ideologies of organizations allocating resources have on the distribution of life chances for people in the urban system. Having done this we would then be able to understand the constraints which people face when they try to obtain the services they require from the agencies [9]. We move one step back in this study and, while we outline the ideologies and goals of organizations and suggest how these can act as constraints facing people, we also concentrate on what the constraints facing *organizations* tell us about the constraints facing people.

Organizational constraints are divisible into two groups. Firstly, there are problems of getting the resources the organization needs in order to operate—for instance money, land, and staff. Secondly, each agency either has to answer to other organizations or groups of people for what it does, or is at least involved with others in doing its job. We discuss where we can the nature of these relationships and point out how they can restrict the activities of the housing agencies. For instance housing associations not only have the usual problem that all agencies have—finding money—they also have to obtain it from a local authority whose co-operation is not necessarily forthcoming. Similarly building societies are accountable not only to the Chief Registrar of Friendly Societies but also to investors. Likewise local authorities are answerable not only to central government but they also try to act in accordance with locally-determined criteria of need and demand.

The various constraints have policy implications if housing needs are to be met more effectively. Policy makers will have to act very differently if it is the problems organizations face in implementing their ideologies rather than their ideologies in themselves which are creating difficulties for 'comprehensive' policies. Such knowledge enables policy makers to draw conclusions concerning whether, for example, organizations need more money, or whether more fundamental changes are required.

In the next six chapters we examine each organization in turn, firstly giving some background information on the kind of agency being examined, secondly, outlining the specific aims of the agencies we looked at, thirdly, discussing the problems they faced in implementing their policies, fourthly, where we collected data, looking at those whom each agency was able to assist,[5] and lastly, discussing the implications of our findings on each agency for 'comprehensive' housing policies. The concluding chapter picks up the general theme of diversity within the organization of housing by exploring the implications of our study for organizational change and more effective housing policies.

References

1. DONNISON, D. 'No more reports', *New Society*, 27 May, 1971.

2. Ministry of Housing and Local Government. *The Housing Programme 1965 to 1970*, Cmnd 2838 (London: H.M.S.O., 1965), p. 17.

3. Department of the Environment. *Widening the Choice: The Next Steps in Housing*, Cmnd 5280 (London: H.M.S.O., 1973), p. 13.

4. See NEVITT, D. and RHODES, G. *The New Government of London, The First Five Years*. G. Rhodes (editor) (London: Weidenfeld and Nicolson, 1972).

5. Standing Working Party on London Housing. *London's Housing Needs up to 1974* (London: Ministry of Housing and Local Government, 1970). Report No. 3, p. 1.

6. *Report of the Committee on the Rent Acts*. Cmnd 4609 (London: H.M.S.O., 1971), pp. 289–98.

7. Greater London Development Plan (GLDP). *Written Statement*, para. 3.20 (London: GLC, 1969).

8. Labour Party Manifesto. *A Socialist Strategy for London:* GLC Election, London, 1973, p. 15.

9. PAHL, R. E. *Urban Sociology and Planning, Urban Social Theory and Research*, Centre for Environmental Studies, University Working Paper 5 (London: 1969).

---

[5] Details of the samples we took are contained in the appendix on methodology where we also discuss our selection of the agencies in more detail and indicate the methodological problems of the study.

Public Enterprise

Chapter One

Local Authorities: Housing to Rent

Background

Unlike most of the housing agencies discussed in this book the geographical area in which the local authorities operate is fixed. This inability to move out of certain areas has important implications for the development and adaptation of local authorities' housing ideologies, for the effect of local needs and political pressure may greatly modify the way in which the political party controlling a given housing authority interprets its party-political predispositions in practice. Thus although the Conservatives nationally have traditionally favoured a residual role and Labour a rather more universalistic role for public housing, their distinct and conflicting approaches are often far less evident in the actual housing policies of Conservative and Labour-controlled local authorities.

When we studied Lambeth, Sutton, and the GLC all three councils were controlled by the Conservatives. However as we shall show in this chapter their policies differed considerably from the uniformity that a mere consideration of their political allegiance might lead one to expect. In the case of Lambeth and Sutton these differences were mainly a product of the differing levels and types of need in the two areas. In Lambeth increased public-sector provision seemed essential and no political dividends could have been gained from policies which disregarded this. In Sutton the need for public housing was less evident and the political climate averse to it. The GLC's position was more complex. The Conservative majority were largely dependent in the long run on political support from outer boroughs such as Sutton but they stayed in power partly because of support from inner boroughs and so faced some of the factors which affected Lambeth's political thinking. The GLC also had a statutory duty under the 1963 London Government Act to have regard to inner as well as outer borough housing problems. So while it could not withdraw from a fairly active public housing role it was reluctant to be as positive in its approach as its Labour predecessor and placed more emphasis than it had done on other, mainly private-sector solutions to London's housing problems.

Aims and Operations of the Local Authorities

Lambeth's main objectives were to meet the high level of general housing need created by a shortage of dwellings and at the same time to clear and improve a large number of unfit and short-life properties. Essential elements in achieving this were an expanded public housing programme, a permanent reduction in the resident population, and co-operation with private-sector agencies in the provision and improvement of dwellings. This latter aim was also pursued because of a concern that the borough might otherwise become a one-class, low-income council house area. For both social and economic reasons therefore the aim of trying to achieve some sort of 'social balance' via a diversity of housing tenures was an important goal.

The 4 per cent Housing Survey conducted by the GLC in 1967 had shown that there were 121 000 households in the borough living in only 94 000 dwelling units and that nearly 10 per cent of the dwellings containing 14 100 households had a life of less than seven years. The difference in the nature of these two problems plus an inadequate supply of land and an increasing financial burden meant that there were no easy solutions. Nevertheless Lambeth attempted to confront the problems by evolving a comprehensive approach to housing which incorporated as many agencies and used as many options as possible. This approach was supported by both parties when in power. Lambeth was concerned to balance the housing revenue account (HRA) as far as possible and not put too much burden on the rates. However, regardless of the party in power, this was not a prime determinant of housing policy after the mid-1960s.[1]

The existence of the bipartisan political consensus on housing policy during 1965-71 must be attributed partly to the role of the Housing Manager, Harry Simpson, who was appointed in 1962. In 1964 he persuaded the Labour leader to tour the borough with the then visiting Milner Holland Committee.[2] This was a foretaste of the way Simpson was to work with politicians to try to encourage them to increase investment in housing. While the Labour Party was in power he worked with the Leader of the Council rather than the Housing Chairman since the Chairman's views remained opposed to increasing development. Lambeth's slum-clearance programme and seven-year building programme were subsequently increased,[3] and the GLC was asked to increase its programme of clearance and nominations for the borough.[4] The Conservatives won the 1968 local election; nevertheless continuity was maintained in housing policy by the Housing Manager despite the fact that the Conservative election manifesto had promised to cut the housing programme, raise rents, sell council houses, and increase the private enterprise contribution.

The leadership structure within the Conservative Party created very powerful committee Chairmen. The Leader was

---

[1] In the first half of the 1960s however, the controlling Labour Party had pursued a policy of 'housing for the working classes' at cheap rents and low cost. The building programme was calculated by assessing firstly, what rate fund contribution the council wanted to pay (which by 1962 was an annual amount of £30 000). Secondly, what the deficiency per dwelling was (£100) and then dividing the first figure by the second. This resulted in a programme of 300 dwellings in 1962 increasing to 500 per annum in 1964. The whole issue of decay in the private sector was ignored.

[2] Which wrote the *Report of the Committee on Housing in Greater London*, Cmnd 2605 (London: H.M.S.O., 1965).

[3] The slum-clearance programme 1966-70 was increased to include 2132 properties and the seven-year rolling programme was updated in 1968 from the average of 720 buildings per annum to a target of 1500 dwellings per annum by 1972.

[4] The GLC carries out two main housing activities which help London boroughs. The first is slum-clearance and redevelopment in consultation with the boroughs in their area. The second is making vacancies available on GLC estates and on some Outer London borough estates.

elected but he then appointed all the chairmen and they were directly accountable to him. It was Peter Cary (the Housing Chairman) and Bernard Perkins (the Leader) who had therefore to be convinced of the need for an expanded building programme. Shortly after the election Simpson took Cary on a tour of some of Brixton's housing and presented him with the results of the GLC survey showing the gross housing deficiency in the borough. Cary persuaded Perkins as a result of this that they must rethink their policy on housing and the party's subsequent document on housing aimed at a target of 2000 new completions per year utilizing all possible agencies, and 1000 converted units, and finally an additional 1000 improved units [1].

The change of outlook was accompanied by a large-scale reorganization within the council after 1968. Services were grouped together under Directors who met once every committee cycle. Policy matters were evolved in this meeting and were forwarded as recommendations from all the Directors. Each committee chairman sat on the Policy Committee (plus the Leader and three other members). Estimates were produced by the Policy Committee of the global total of expenditure and the targets for each committee. A planning, programming and budgeting system[5] and a $7\frac{1}{2}$ per cent growth rate in expenditure was permitted for other services. Despite this housing expenditure had achieved a 20 per cent annual growth rate by 1971. The Leader of the Council, Perkins, had always been interested in the provision and expansion of the social services but his priorities when in office became housing first, social services second, and he felt that until the housing situation was improved many of the problems in the social services would remain. He felt that having good housing was

---

[5] PPBS is an attempt to 'analyse expenditure according to the purpose for which it is to be spent and relate it to the results achieved . . . the system is designed to expose choices for policy decision both within the programme areas and between them . . . there are, however, three other main elements . . . programme analysis, the process whereby objectives and alternative ways of achieving them are examined and compared with the resources required . . . multi-year planning of expenditure, feedback, and review of performance'. From *Lambeth Community Plan 1972–1977*. General Preface, Lambeth Borough Council, London, 1972.

good preventive social work. In 1970 Cary moved to the Chairmanship of the Finance Committee, where he was able to sustain investment in housing and the new Housing Chairman, John Major, supported the Leader's priorities.

Reorganization went on simultaneously within the Housing Directorate to enable a comprehensive approach to housing to be implemented. Authority was vested in the Director of Housing and the Director of Finance, instead of the previous Housing Loans sub-committee, to approve advances for the purchase, construction, and improvement of dwellings by individuals or housing associations. Public Health Inspectors became part of the Directorate in order to look after the extended registration scheme for houses in multiple occupation[6] and to play a significant part in the general improvement area decision making. They were given as much delegated authority as possible. In 1970 a Housing Advice Centre was opened as a front-line medium for contact with the public. Applicants to the Advice Centre were encouraged to leave Lambeth where possible because of the shortage of land and housing. To further this approach the council's mortgage scheme was made available for the purchase of property outside the borough and the council had developed links with twenty other local authorities and new towns which would provide housing if employment was found. An experiment in by-passing the delays of the Industrial Selection Scheme[7] was carried out by holding a 'Peterborough Week' at the Advice Centre, to provide information on housing and job opportunities in that

---

[6] In 1965 the Labour council decided to keep a register of houses in multiple occupation, for the six central wards of the borough. It was to apply to (a) any house which, or part of which, was let in lodgings, and occupied by more than one family; (b) any building comprising separate dwellings two or more of which did not have a w.c. and personal washing facilities accessible only to those living in the dwelling. In 1970 this scheme was made more stringent and extended to the whole borough.

[7] The ISS is an administrative scheme which links workers in housing need in the conurbations with supply of housing and jobs in the new and expanding towns. It involves the participation of the local authorities in the conurbations, the new and expanding town authorities, employers, and the Department of Employment. In London the scheme is co-ordinated by the GLC. The cumbrousness of this procedure and its ineffectiveness have been widely criticized.

new town.[8] Owner occupiers, landlords, and property managers were encouraged to come to the Advice Centre for help in obtaining 'fair rents', improvement grants, and information about financial assistance and loans from the council. Meetings were held with building societies in order to try to persuade them to liberalize their lending policies and help in the process of improvement and stimulating owner occupation. The Director thought that the lower interest rates building societies charge in comparison with other sources of finance could make a significant difference to the ability and willingness of people to take part in the improvement of properties particularly in 'General Improvement Areas' (GIAs). By the end of 1971 the council were planning 50 GIAs covering 19 000 dwellings, approximately 20 per cent of the housing stock.

Thus Lambeth's programme did not concentrate solely on house-building. Its policy was multifaceted, aiming to use all its possible options in a comprehensive manner. The programme envisaged that 500 of the target 2000 new dwellings should be provided by private enterprise and half of the 1000 converted units were to be provided by housing associations, in order to maintain the council's goal of achieving 'social balance' in the community.

We have pointed out that the idea of a comprehensive housing policy was emphasized by central government which expected local authorities to adopt it. But the degree to which local authorities identified with the ideas differed considerably.

Sutton presents a marked contrast to Lambeth both in terms of housing policy and in terms of its organization. Public housing was regarded as a residual provision for those who could not find private-sector solutions and these people were not expected to be a rapidly growing proportion of the borough's inhabitants. Measures were taken to help private development and owner occupation where this seemed possible and housing associations were encouraged to provide for the

---

[8] *Lambeth to Peterborough: a report on Peterborough Week in Lambeth* (Peterborough Development Corporation and London Borough of Lambeth, London, 1971). 496 families said they would like to live in Peterborough. Twelve months after the 'special week', 46 families had been found jobs; 21 were skilled workers, 13 semi-skilled, 3 unskilled, and the remainder were white-collar workers and foremen.

one large sector of the population, the elderly, which appeared from the borough waiting list to be in considerable need but unable to buy their own house. More public housing was thought to be socially disadvantageous and its expansion resisted. A central goal of Sutton's housing policy was to make the housing revenue account 'self-supporting'. The council decided in 1965 that the only exception to this would be that 'unremunerative loan charges'[9] would be met by a rate fund contribution which would be recouped to the general rate fund within nine years. In addition deficiencies arising from the provision of dwellings for the elderly would be met from the general rate fund. Rent rebates, however, were to be met from the housing revenue account not the general rate fund. Initially they aimed at keeping rent increases stable for three years but when this proved irreconcilable with the goal of making the housing revenue account self-balancing rents were raised to 100 per cent GV[10] in 1965, and 150 per cent GV in 1967, to 175 per cent GV for new tenants and 162 per cent GV for all others, in January 1970, and finally to $187\frac{1}{2}$ per cent GV for new tenancies and $182\frac{1}{2}$ per cent GV for all others in 1967. The rent rebate scheme was slightly adjusted each time, but the protests of the Joint Tenant's Consultative Council at the increases were ineffective.[11]

Apart from minimizing rate fund contributions for housing the council was also keen to contain the growth in the proportion of council-owned dwellings, and to confine council building to certain parts of the borough only. In 1967 council housing in Sutton was 18 per cent of the total stock and the

---

[9] i.e. charges payable on sites during the period between the start of development and the receipt of rents.

[10] Gross value—the imputed rent obtained from the property, a valuation technique used for rating purposes.

[11] The Joint Tenants' Consultative Council, a borough-wide organization of Tenants' Associations demanded, in 1965:

(a) the rescinding of rent increases,

(b) that rebates should come from the general rate fund,

(c) interest rates be fixed at $2\frac{1}{2}$ per cent,

(d) maximum rents be fixed nationally, and

(e) decoration and repairs should be the borough's responsibility.

Demonstrations of 300 tenants and 1000 tenants were held in April and July 1967 respectively.

Leader of the Council had decided that 20–25 per cent was to be the maximum. It was criteria such as these rather than criteria of need which determined the size of the council building programme. By 1970 the council were becoming worried about the proportion of the total housing stock that council housing would eventually comprise[12] and they decided that each application for council housing should be examined to see if need could be met as far as practicable by the 'miscellaneous properties'[13] owned by the council, and that a more positive and vigorous policy regarding under-occupation should be adopted in the future.

Sutton borough was formed in 1965 from the amalgamation of Sutton and Cheam, Carshalton, and Beddington and Wallington. The constituent parts of the borough however still retained their individual identity despite amalgamation. Sutton council relied for the bulk of its Conservative support on Sutton and Cheam. In fact only slightly less than half the total members were Conservatives from Sutton and Cheam and thus they tended to control the chairmanships of council committees. Carshalton had always had a much higher proportion of council dwellings than either Beddington and Wallington or Sutton and Cheam, largely because of the presence of the GLC St Helier estate in Carshalton,[14] and was the main centre of

---

[12] After allowing for the council property which would be transferred from the GLC to the borough in accordance with the first phase of the arrangements in the 1963 London Government Act, which envisaged the transfer of all but a strategic reserve of the GLC housing stock to the boroughs, after a transitional period, the number of council-owned dwellings was expected to reach 16 240 by 1981, 24 per cent of the projected total housing stock of 67 200.

[13] These are properties acquired by councils as a result of their other activities rather than being purpose-built in execution of the local authorities' housing responsibilities.

[14]

Households in local authority dwellings	LA	Total HH	LA as percentage of total
Beddington and Wallington MB	958	10 927	8·7
Carshalton U.D.	17 135	17 925	39·6
Sutton and Cheam	1300	26 630	4·8

Source: 1961 Census.

Labour support. The council accepted that the borough would have to take the initiative in redevelopment in the northern parts of the borough, which included some other areas which private developers would not find an attractive prospect. But on the other hand, council housing was not deemed suitable for the southern part of the borough, South Cheam, Belmont, and South Sutton. Significantly it was only in this higher status part of the borough that any real development planning was being undertaken, in co-operation with the council's development control section, so as to maintain the high amenity of the area.[15] In order to preserve the *status quo* of the different areas of the borough, to contain the proportion of council development, and to minimize the deficit to be met from the rates, the council tried to redevelop old low-density council estates in Beddington rather than buy expensive land. The estates had been built early in the twentieth century and there was very little outstanding debt left on them. However the Minister refused his consent on the grounds that the estates could be improved and were not obsolete.

The fact that Sutton did not regard its housing functions as a universalist social service but rather as a residual provision for those unable to cater for themselves was reflected in the organization and status of the housing department and its chief officers. Housing had never been a separate department of first-rank status and housing policy evolved as a result of decisions which were primarily made by other Chief Officers and council committees. Even in 1965 when there was a separate housing department headed by a Chief Officer and the Housing Committee was one of the ten council committees, the powers of the Committee were restricted. The erection, rebuilding or alteration of buildings costing more than £5000 needed council authorization and the Committee had little say in the amount to be contributed to the HRA from the rate

---

[15] The area concerned was South Cheam, which housed many of the local 'establishment'. Two houses at £20 000 each came on to the market in 1967 and the prospective developers had been planning to reduce the size of the gardens. The development control section of the Planning Department wanted to maintain the quality of the area so they insisted on minimum frontage and landscape requirements. A public meeting was held and 400 people of the locality attended and gave the Department their approval.

fund. Rent policy was decided by the council on the basis of the Borough Treasurer's estimate of the future deficit on the housing revenue account. The scope of housing policy which the Chief Officers could recommend to the committee was limited by the elected members' decision that the HRA must be broadly self-supporting.

In 1967 there was a reorganization of council committees and housing management was subsumed within the Directorate of Health and Family Services of which the Medical Officer of Health was Director. The Housing Manager lost his Chief Officer status and also his responsibility for housing maintenance which was assumed by the Borough Architect. In 1969 the function of rent collection became the Borough Treasurer's responsibility although the administration of rebates remained the responsibility of the Housing Department. In April 1971, the Housing Manager was again made a Chief Officer within the Health and Family Services Department, on a par with the Medical Officer of Health and Director of Social Services. Nevertheless housing remained stripped of some of its responsibilities and this complicated the housing management function.

A similar ideology pervaded all the council committees and the differences between the various committees on housing policy were few. In 1968 when the council committees were reorganized a Management Committee (the equivalent of a policy committee) was established with the responsibility of recommending to the council their major objectives and the policies for achieving these; resolving conflicting decisions of functional committees, and appointing Chief Officers. All committees made recommendations to the Management Committee which in turn made recommendations to the council. Thus the existence of the Management Committee ensured the co-ordination of policy. Furthermore the Chairman of the Management Committee had also been leader of the Conservative majority during the whole period of the authority's existence. The chairmen of all committees were appointed by him and he was also an *ex officio* member of all committees.

As we saw above, Lambeth too had a structure which was tightly controlled by the Leader and a Policy Committee. But in Sutton Chief Officers did not play the same kind of role as they did in Lambeth and there was little scope for new initiatives from them. The Leader of the Council made it clear when interviewed that Chief Officers were there solely to suggest alternatives, not to take a stance. Contrast this with the situation in Lambeth where the Chairman of the Housing Committee stated that sometimes it was difficult to tell who was Housing Director and who was Committee Chairman.

Throughout the evolution of housing policy in Sutton the Treasurer's role was as important, if not more so, than that of the Chief Housing Officer. The Borough Treasurer's Annual Reports on the state of the HRA were instrumental in prompting the Health and Family Services Committee to recommend rent policy changes whereas the periodic reports by the Chief Housing Officer on the stock of dwellings and the characteristics of the waiting list did not necessarily result in policy changes.

Thus since Sutton's housing policy was not determined primarily by assessments of housing need, its attitude towards the housing problems of Inner London was predictable. Sutton consistently opposed the idea that the GLC should assume positive overall responsibility for housing in London. During the period when it was Labour controlled, the GLC had recommended, in the light of the Milner Holland Report,[16] that it should go into partnership with the London boroughs to renovate the twilight areas and that it should take maximum advantage of the Outer London boroughs both by building there and by nomination arrangements. They also recommended that the London boroughs should buy under-occupied dwellings. Sutton sharply disagreed with all these proposals but agreed to make available to the GLC 15 per cent of the dwellings completed each year as part of its four-year housing programme,[17] on the condition that during the period in which the arrangements were operative the GLC would not seek to acquire land or properties within the borough for housing

---

[16] See Milner Holland, op. cit., ch. 13, p. 228, points 10 and 12.
[17] Under the terms, the GLC agreed to pay for fifteen years to the borough council the net annual cost of the dwellings and a contribution equivalent to the interest charges incurred during their construction. The net annual cost is the debt charges, contributions to the repairs and renewals fund, the cost of supervision and management, minus Exchequer subsidy and rent. Sutton reserved the right to accept or reject families nominated by the GLC.

purposes, except after consultation and with the agreement of the council.

When one of the minority party spokesmen asked the Health and Family Services Committee Chairman in 1969 whether the council would get down to providing more homes for other Londoners on the waiting list in the GLC area, the Chairman stated,

'I do not consider we were elected to solve the GLC's housing problems. Our primary function is to solve the housing problems in Sutton with the GLC's problem being of secondary importance thereto.'[18]

This was indeed the basis of the 1963 London Government Act which had set up the boroughs and the GLC in 1965. The result was that the actual number of dwellings allocated to the GLC by Sutton amounted to 20 in 1967, 43 in 1968, 72 in 1969, 67 in 1970, and 111 in 1971.

When Professor Cullingworth [2] was asked to investigate the implications of the transfer of the GLC estates to the boroughs, Sutton submitted a memorandum of evidence in line with the thinking behind the 1963 Act, namely that housing management should be as local a service as possible, and undertaken by the same authority that was administering the personal health and social services. Sutton thought it unnecessary for the GLC to retain its own pool of housing and considered its statutory housing obligations should be met by the right to claim nominations. In this they concurred with the general views of the London Boroughs' Association on the transfer.

Nevertheless the borough was keen to appear to show some concern for Inner London, due partly to the fact that the Conservative Leader was Chairman (and in 1972 was Deputy Chairman) of the London Boroughs Association,[19] and was also

---

[18] Question by Councillor Goodall of Councillor Martin. Sutton Minutes, 15 May, 1969.

[19] The LBA is a body consisting of representatives of all the London boroughs served by officers drawn from all these areas. Its purposes are to co-ordinate policies and represent the collective interests of the boroughs as a whole and to discuss problems which affect these boroughs and their relationships with each other, the GLC, central government and other bodies. It is London's version of the older established local authority associations.

a member of the LBA's special committee on housing. When the council decided that it would create too much of a burden on the housing revenue account to develop part of a site released by the Air Ministry, it offered it to the GLC to develop in conjunction with that part of the site which the GLC was already proposing to develop. This was done on the basis that the borough council would have nomination rights and that the whole development would eventually be transferred to the borough when Phase 1 of the proposed handover of GLC housing to the boroughs envisaged in the 1963 London Government Act occurred. By April 1970 however the GLC decided against proceeding unless the borough council were prepared to pay full capital costs on completion in the event of a transfer. The borough therefore decided to make the land available to private developers or housing associations, and in future to permit only private or housing association development in the interests of keeping the publicly owned proportion of the housing stock down to the level of 20–25 per cent. Finally in 1971 the Conservative majority maintained that they offered an increased percentage of nominations to the GLC which was refused.[20] In the past the high rent levels of Sutton's dwellings could well have made their offers unattractive to some GLC nominees.

Sutton Council decided to restrict council house building in the seventies to two categories of need—old people and the physically handicapped. By 1972, 30–40 acres of land were earmarked for sale to private enterprise. We shall see in subsequent chapters how this ideology of maximizing home ownership and minimizing public building has affected the council's mortgage scheme and how the council endeavoured to encourage developers to build cheap houses.

Of the three local authorities the goals of the Greater London Council are the most complex to discuss. The break in political continuity which occurred when the Conservatives gained control in 1967 was accompanied by a change in the goals of the GLC. This is in contrast to the change of political control in Lambeth in 1968 which did not lead to a change in policy but rather to a more vigorous implementation of the goals of

[20] Appendix to Council Minutes, 1 April, 1971.

the preceding Labour majority. It contrasts too with the situation in Sutton, where continuous Conservative control meant that a consistent theme ran through housing policy during the period under study.

The formal limits of the GLC's powers are laid down in the London Government Act 1963. Under the Act the thirty-two new London boroughs became the primary housing authorities within their areas. The GLC retains certain permanent powers including the provision of housing in comprehensive development areas under the Planning Acts, the rehousing of persons displaced by the GLC in consequence of action it takes in the exercise of any of its powers, and the provision of housing in Greater London for other purposes, subject to the consent of the London borough in whose area it proposed to provide the housing, or if that consent is withheld, the consent of the Minister. Finally the GLC is the sole London authority for the provision of housing outside Greater London and for the purpose of the Town Development Act 1952.[21] Because the GLC retains these permanent powers, it has a duty under the 1957 Housing Act[22] 'to consider housing conditions in their district and the needs of the district with respect to the provision of further housing accommodation', and to submit to the Minister proposals for the provision of new houses.

In addition, the London Government Act gave the GLC all the housing powers of the previous LCC on a transitional basis until such date as the Minister should decide that the transitional period was ended. These transitional arrangements were devised 'in order to maintain the impetus of the housing effort in Greater London and to give time for the permanent arrangements to be worked out'.[23] The GLC was given transitional authority for undertaking slum-clearance in Inner London, so that the GLC and the twelve inner boroughs have concurrent powers under Part III of the 1957 Housing Act. Despite Sir Keith Joseph's original expectation that the transitional powers of the GLC would be terminated by 1970, the subsequent Labour government decided against this.

---

[21] An act enabling existing towns to receive overspill population and industry from the conurbations.
[22] S.91 1957 Housing Act and S.21 of London Government Act 1963.
[23] MHLG Circular 1/65, S.3, 20 January, 1965.

The shortcomings of the 1963 London Government Act as a means of dealing with London's housing problems have been concisely pointed out by Barry Cullingworth [2]. In theory the GLC's duty was clear. In practical terms it should have involved considering the total need in London and then the extent to which that need was likely to be met by the London borough councils and by private enterprise and therefore how many dwellings it ought to provide each year in the interests of London as a whole. In fact the ideological predispositions of the political parties controlling the GLC during this period and the pattern of political control of the thirty-two London borough councils affected the way in which this was interpreted.

The Conservative central government envisaged the new system working on the basis of co-operation between the GLC and the London boroughs, but during 1965–67 the GLC was controlled by a Labour majority. The Labour-controlled LCC had always been committed to the concept of the new and expanding towns, the decentralization of London's population, and the reduction of densities within Inner London. The role of the GLC in redistributing population and industry still appeared important to the Labour majority in 1965. In the wake of Milner Holland's revelations about the increasing housing stress in certain inner boroughs Keith Joseph's hopes about inter-borough co-operation appeared to be quite inadequate as far as the Labour councillors were concerned. Hence one of the first things Evelyn Denington did as Labour Chairman of the Housing Committee was to cajole the Outer London boroughs into making over a percentage of their new building for Inner London's needs. All but six of the twenty outer boroughs concluded agreements giving the GLC the right to nominate tenants to a proportion (usually 10 per cent) of new dwellings built by the borough. Five of the six outer boroughs (Barking, Brent, Haringey, Newham, and Waltham Forest) all had considerable housing problems of their own and were actually beneficiaries under this scheme with the Inner London boroughs. The sixth, Hounslow, preferred a policy of encouraging the GLC to build within the borough rather than the GLC having the right of nomination to borough dwellings. This was in contrast to a number of other boroughs (e.g. Croydon, Richmond, and Hillingdon) which stipulated in return for nomination agreements that no building should be undertaken within their borough boundaries by the GLC. [3]

The advent of the Conservative majority was accompanied by significant changes in housing and planning policy. While in opposition the Conservatives had stressed their commitment to increasing the role of private enterprise in the provision of housing in London.[24] Once in control of the council they shifted the emphasis in GLC housing policy, encouraging the development of housing associations and enhancing the role of local authority mortgages for increased owner occupation. Council housing was to be a final resort for those unable to obtain housing through any other means and the objective of reducing the rate subsidy to the housing revenue account became one of the determinants of housing policy.

The GLC delegated powers where it could and the Conservatives set up a Chief Officers' Board with six other Boards representing specific policy areas. In addition PPBS was introduced as in Lambeth. Other departmental and committee changes were designed mainly to strengthen the planning functions of the GLC and to help produce the Greater London Development Plan but also to strengthen the political control of policy making along the lines of the predominant Conservative party philosophy. A Leader's Co-ordinating Committee was introduced as well as a Policy Steering Committee both giving a few members of the majority party supreme control.

In December 1967 the Conservatives estimated that a 70 per cent average increase in rents would eliminate the need for a rate fund subsidy to the housing revenue account. They were committed to increasing rents to 'fair rent' level and estimated that an increase of between 60–100 per cent would bring GLC rents into line with fair rents in the private sector.[25]

It was partly the desire to make the housing revenue account self-balancing and to increase private enterprise's role in the

---

[24] See, for example, debate in the GLC on the Milner Holland Report, GLC Minutes, 14 December, 1965.

[25] This estimated increase of 60–100 per cent was arrived at somewhat unsatisfactorily. The council visited Rent Officers but did not gain complete co-operation. The estimated increase was based on those areas that did co-operate and was thereby not necessarily representative of Greater London as a whole.

provision of housing in London, that accounted for the sharp drop in the amount of land acquired by the GLC for its land bank once the Conservatives assumed control.[26] Admittedly too the drop in the land acquired reflected the fact that there was a diminishing amount of land available for housing in Greater London. The greater part of the land acquired between 1965–67 consisted of 'once and for all' opportunity sites such as Thamesmead, the Lee Valley, and Croydon Airport. Shortage of land was becoming a real constraint but it coincided with the political predisposition of the GLC which probably would have been decisive on its own. Attempts by some of the Inner London boroughs in 1972 to acquire land in the outer boroughs were discouraged by the GLC.

The Problems the Authorities Faced

Given the different aims of the three authorities, what were the differences in the problems they faced and how were their aims actually impeded by circumstances and prevented from being implemented in their original form? The main constraints were land, finance, and the attitudes of other boroughs. The importance of each of these three constraints varied both quantitively and qualitatively according to the housing ideology of our authorities.

One of the problems which the Sutton housing department encountered was the outdated borough plan on which policies were based. Sutton Planning Department was still using the 1958 Initial Development Plan for their part of Surrey. This was mainly a description of land use rather than a strategy

26

Year	Acres	Dwellings which could be built
1965–66	920	19 500
1966–67	650	13 100
1967–68	130	5100
1968–69	145	3700
1969–70	95	3000
1970–71	99	2000

Source: GLC Minutes, 23 February, 1971 and 22 June, 1971.

for development. Therefore up-to-date information on land available for development was difficult for other departments to obtain. In addition over half the 200 acres which was suitable for housing development, according to the Leader of the Council, was owned by other boroughs (Merton and Croydon) and had to be re-zoned for residential use by the GLC, which the GLC had not yet done, or was owned by Ministries or British Rail. However, although Sutton had the disadvantage of not controlling much of the available land and had to wait on other agencies' consent, in fact it had no reason to push as hard as it might have done for the release of land.

The GLC was in a similar position. It too was constrained by lack of land as we have just seen but this coincided with their policy not to intervene in London's house-building programme to an extent which went much beyond the clearance it was already undertaking in Inner London. The GLC was certainly constrained by the powers given it by the London Government Act. Both the Herbert Commission and the London Government Act linked housing with personal health and welfare services, and thereby made the boroughs the primary housing authorities. The links between housing and planning were not explicitly discussed anywhere in the Herbert Commission's report. The result was that although the GLC did not use its powers to the full, it was undeniably hindered by the outlook of the Outer London boroughs. An average of about 850 dwellings a year was made available by Outer London boroughs in their percentage nomination agreements with the GLC. The contributions depended on the size of the borough's own building programmes since most of the agreements were in terms of a percentage of new dwellings. Hence the GLC was powerless when some of the Outer London boroughs severely reduced their building programme after 1967 and the nomination quota dropped accordingly. By 1970 the Conservative-controlled GLC acknowledged that its duty under the 1957 Housing Act entailed considering the total need in London, and then deciding how many dwellings it ought to provide each year in the interests of London as a whole, depending on how many the boroughs provided. However it stressed that

'the proportion of total demand that the GLC must deal with in the discharge of its role is difficult to assess because no firm long-term forecasts are available of the production of new houses by the borough councils as primary authorities'.[27]

The fact that many Housing Managers in outer boroughs such as Sutton, were second-tier officers and had far less power than their Inner London counterparts put the GLC at a further disadvantage in its negotiations.

Finally both Sutton and the GLC found that their rent policies were constrained by the actions of the then Labour government under its prices and incomes legislation. In April 1966 Sutton wanted to raise rents to 150 per cent GV but the Leader of the Labour opposition reported this to the government and the increase was deferred until January 1967. A condition of the rise being allowed was that another should not occur for two years. Rents were then increased again but a further attempt to increase them in the summer of 1970 was refused by the outgoing Labour administration and subsequently the new government only allowed a limited increase. Similarly the GLC had their first stage of increases towards 'fair rents' limited to an average of 37½p in 1967 (they had wanted 57½p) and were prohibited altogether when trying for a second increase in 1969.[28] In 1970 a further rise was allowed and by 1971 it was estimated that rents had risen on average by about 50 per cent. The advent of the Conservative government marked the beginning of a phase where the GLC and the Ministry were in basic agreement over rent policy which was to be crystallized in the White Paper 'Fair Deal for Housing'. Meanwhile the GLC had decided that, although complete parity with 'fair rents' in the private sector would not be possible during the ensuing three years, rents would nevertheless be generally increased to the 1971 'fair rent' level.

Of the three authorities, Lambeth was constrained to the greatest extent in its attempts to translate its public-sector aims into practice. It was hindered both by the lack of resources within its own territory, and by the fact that its aims depended on the co-operation of the other two authorities whose own aims did not coincide with Lambeth's. Since its comprehensive ideology was different from that of Sutton and the GLC the

---

[27] GLC Minutes, 27 January, 1970.
[28] GLC Minutes, 16 January, 1969.

constraints on land, finance, and co-operation had a different qualitative meaning.

The shortage and high-price of land affected Lambeth acutely. The clearance of sites for redevelopment to make a housing 'gain' became the main hope of eventually overcoming the housing shortage. This meant that the council had to rehouse more families in the new dwellings on a given site than it displaced when demolishing the old. The degree of housing need in the borough was not known exactly but it was thought to be far more extensive than the waiting list suggested.[29] Any policy of making a housing 'gain' could not include areas of overcrowding or sharing initially. The borough therefore chose areas of unfit rather than short-life, overcrowded housing for clearance. But, as the remaining areas of unfit housing got smaller, so more and more short-life properties had to be included in the compulsory purchase orders in order to demolish sufficient dwellings to make an adequate area for new building. But there was a limit to the proportion of these 'grey lands' (not being unfit) which could be added to a compulsory purchase order on unfit housing and gain Ministerial approval. Usually only up to 50 per cent of the original area was allowed in 'added lands'. Therefore the council had to rely increasingly on Part V of the Housing Act in order to be allowed to clear fit properties, arguing that such action was necessary in order to meet general housing needs.

Usually a council has to show that a housing gain will be made before the Minister will approve a Part V order.[30] But

---

[29] There were 13 500 families on the waiting list and the figure was increasing by 200–300 per month. But in one area, consisting of four-storey houses in multiple occupation to be compulsorily purchased by the council, it was found that, despite the terribly poor living conditions, only 14 per cent of families had placed their names on the waiting list.

[30] Under Part III of the Housing Act 1957, a local authority can decide to clear an area where it is satisfied that the housing is unfit for human habitation. The authority may also purchase any land which is surrounded by the clearance area and the acquisition of which 'is reasonably necessary for the purpose of securing a cleared area of convenient shape and dimensions and any adjoining land the acquisition of which is reasonably necessary for the satisfactory development or use of the clearance area'—'grey lands'. Under Part V of the 1957 Act, a local authority has a duty to consider housing conditions and the needs of its

Lambeth found that it was difficult to produce housing gains from areas of short-life fit housing because they were likely to have more households per dwelling than older unfit houses. Ministerial encouragement of rehabilitation and improvement, rather than redevelopment, did not by the end of the 1960s improve matters in this respect either.[31] The emphasis on General Improvement Areas made it harder to find sites for development. Moreover the declaration of overcrowded sites as GIAs still meant that there was an overspill which it was difficult to deal with, given the overall shortage of land in the borough. By the early 1970s it became clear that, whatever strategy was employed, it was becoming virtually impossible for Lambeth to provide houses within its own boundaries for all who wanted or needed them. Part III and Part V sites with overspill were outnumbering those with a gain and available land was rapidly decreasing. It was estimated that, by 1977–78, there would still be 15 000 households in Lambeth without a separate dwelling and that there would then be less than 100 acres (which could lead to the construction of approximately 3000 dwellings, at a density of 100 persons per acre) still available for redevelopment.

The growing deficit on the housing revenue account as a result of the increased building programme necessitated frequent rent increases. In 1965 the Labour Party had increased rents to 1.0 GV, by 1967[32] it was aware of the need for further increases but refrained from implementing them because of the

---

district with respect to the provision of further accommodation. Land with houses which are not unfit can be compulsorily acquired and demolished provided that the needs of the area justify it and that more houses will be constructed as a result.

[31] Lambeth's neighbour, Southwark, had a Part III order turned down by the Minister on the grounds that the dwellings were capable of repair at reasonable cost (but this does not appear to be a legally valid reason for refusing such an order).

[32] The actual deficiency for 1966–67 was £964 290. The estimated deficits for 1967–68 and 1968–69 were £1 225 000 and £1 675 000. A considerable part of the increase was due to increased debt charges. The problem was that, despite the subsidies available under the 1967 Housing Subsidies Act, loans obtained under previous Acts had to be refinanced at higher rates of interest. In addition building costs had increased, together with the cost of supervision, management, maintenance and repair.

impending elections. By 1969 the Conservative-controlled council decided to introduce 'fair rents', 1.5 GV for pre-war dwellings, 1.6 GV for post-war and 2.1 GV for 'Parker Morris'[33] dwellings but increased the rebate scheme at the same time.[34] The total additional income estimated from the new rent increases, after allowing for changes in the rebate scheme, was £103 000 for 1968–69 and £385 000 for 1969–70. Compared to the actual overall deficit of £2.4m by 1971, rent increases plus suitable amendments in the rebate scheme could come nowhere near solving Lambeth's problems. On the other hand these sharp increases meant that, for example, by 1970–71 Lambeth was charging more than all but two other London boroughs for a post-1964 three-bedroomed flat. [4] It seemed likely that some families, which were eligible for rehousing by the council but were not eligible for a rebate, were leaving the borough in order to buy. The effects of such a movement, apart from making the public sector socially 'imbalanced' would be to force out the very families that could afford the new rents thereby undermining two goals of the Housing Department—'social balance' and the reduction of the financial deficit. By 1971, 52 per cent of families in newly let accommodation received rebates.

Unlike the situation in Sutton and the GLC the obligation to keep rates down was not an overriding concern but it was important. Cary obtained the consent of the rest of the party to an expanded building programme on condition that the rate would not increase by more than $12\frac{1}{2}$p in five years.[35] He admitted that with housing as top priority they could not hope to reduce the £1.4m deficit borne by the rates, especially because of the high interest burden on the extensive amount of

---

[33] The Parker Morris Report, *Homes for Today and Tomorrow* (London: H.M.S.O., 1961), recommended improved space and amenities for new council houses. The standards were later accepted by central government.
[34] The ex-chairman of the Housing Committee, Peter Cary, claimed that their 'fair rents' were set by principles similar to those used by the Rent Officer (and the GLC). If so it is difficult to see how the rents set for the three categories of housing could be defined in terms of multiples of gross value.
[35] It increased by $\frac{1}{2}$p 1968–70, but by 11p in the last year of Conservative control.

land being prepared for redevelopment which the large-scale programme required.

Apart from this political dilemma, Lambeth was also impeded by staff shortages. In 1972 it was estimated that an additional twenty-five architects were required if the 1974–75 programme was to succeed. By 1971 the council needed 64 acres per annum for all its land requirements. But it was not until 1970 that it had sufficient staff in the Directorate of Administrative and Legal Services for the land acquisition programme, in particular for the detailed 'referencing' of properties—looking up or tracing the owner and interested parties so that compulsory purchase can proceed. These staffing problems contributed to a 'slip rate' between the approval of the housing programme and the start of construction of 13 per cent in 1966, rising to 20 per cent by 1972. In addition there was an average slip rate of over 40 per cent during the actual period of building caused by labour and material shortages in the building industry—a factor of increasing seriousness in London at this time.

There were a number of solutions to the shortage of land in Lambeth. John Major, the Housing Chairman who replaced Peter Cary, thought it was utterly unrealistic of the Outer London boroughs to refuse to assist Inner London. If they did not agree to planned overspill, they would be faced with an unplanned one. The Planning Directorate however had different views. They were concerned that the people who were able to move out of Lambeth were the most active economically, being forced out both by bad housing opportunities and by the decline of employment. They feared that the Housing Department's future redevelopment programme would further accelerate the decline of manufacturing industry in the borough and accentuate the loss of those 'who contribute much to the social and cultural life of the community'.[36]

The Housing Directorate was not averse to maintaining 'social balance' within the borough for, as we have mentioned, the building programme aimed at a 25 per cent contribution from the private sector. Building societies, private landlords, and other property owners were to be asked to contribute to the

---

[36] *GLDP Enquiry Proof E11/15*; Objector: London Borough of Lambeth, paras 2.7, 3.2, 3.3, and 3.7.

improvement of the stock so as to maintain a diversification of effort, opportunity, and tenure. Housing associations were being encouraged to ensure a further diversification of ownership and to cater for that section of the community which, although unable to provide its own accommodation, is capable of paying high rents. We shall see in the following chapters whether all these aims coincided with the goals of the actual organizations concerned. As far as Lambeth was concerned it expected all these agencies to help solve its housing problems. However, despite these aims, the overriding urgency to solve the shortage meant that the Housing Department encouraged trends that the Planning Department deplored.

We have analysed the aims of the three authorities and described some of the constraints inherent in the total context within which the organizations operate. In the next section we shall see who actually were the beneficiaries of the respective council building programmes.

Who got Housed?

We saw earlier in this chapter how Lambeth pursued a policy of maximizing housing gain. This meant it concentrated on redeveloping areas with the least sharing and overcrowding where the households tended to be older 'controlled' tenants, rather than young newcomers with families in furnished accommodation. As a result Lambeth's building programme was geared to the demands of small households—retired people, and older households where the children had left home. Of the households rehoused by Lambeth between 1965 and 1970, 50 per cent had no children, and 75 per cent of these came from clearance areas.[37]

Compared to Sutton where there was far less pressure, Lambeth's housing strategy was very dependent on the role of the GLC. The system by which Lambeth could nominate families to the GLC became an important source of housing for those families with dependent children that Lambeth, in pursuit of its policy of housing gain, was unable to house itself. Of Lambeth's new tenants 16 per cent had three or more

---

[37] See the Appendix for details of the samples.

children but 34 per cent of Lambeth's nominees to the GLC had families of this size.

Table 1.1

Council Tenants Samples
Number of Children (percentage)

		Lambeth (1965–71)	Sutton (1965–71)	Lambeth nominees to GLC (1970–71)	GLC SDO (1965–71)	GLC* St Helier (1968–71)
Number of children	0	50	26	19	59	36
	1	17	30	15	9	17
	2	16	25	32	14	25
	3	6	12	23	7	18
	4	6	3	7	4	4
	5+	4	1	4	1	—
No information			3		7	
Total %		100	100	100	100	100
N		556	273	142	167	121
Mean = number		1·16	1·36	1·95	0·83	1·37

(Percentages may not add up to 100 because of rounding.)

* For a description of the boundaries of the GLC Southern District Office and the St Helier District Office areas, see the Appendix.

(*Note:* Because Lambeth had bought up many houses in areas of heavy multiple occupation and could thereby have transferred some of these families into new tenancies, we checked the tenants who had been transferred from one council tenancy to another since 1965 in case they included large numbers of households with children. But 64 per cent of transfers had no children and only 13 per cent had three or more children.)

Although a third of the families rehoused by Lambeth in the period came from the waiting list there was no significant difference in family size between these families and those from clearance areas. What is more, the waiting list tenants were also unlikely to have come from areas of multiple occupation with insecure furnished, shared accommodation of the kind to be found in the stress areas where younger but poorer families with children are concentrated. By far the majority of waiting-list applicants came from unfurnished accommodation.[38] The

---

[38] There were difficulties in obtaining completely reliable figures on previous tenure. In Lambeth 37 per cent of tenants were recorded as

major part of this unfurnished accommodation was not likely
to be in multiple occupation but to consist of older controlled
tenancies where the main deficiency was the absence of
facilities like baths, although there was certainly some sharing
going on. But in fact a higher percentage of Sutton waiting-list
applicants housed shared bath and toilet than did those from
the waiting list which were housed by Lambeth. At one time,
as we have already shown, Lambeth found that only 14 per cent
of families in an area of multiple occupation were on the waiting
list.

Table 1.2

Council Tenants Samples
Lambeth and Sutton: Tenants Rehoused from the Waiting List
(percentages in brackets)

Facilities	Lambeth	Sutton
No bath	76 (39)	23 (13)
Share bath	84 (43)	110 (66)
Sole use of bath	33 (17)	32 (19)
No w.c.	6 (3)	5 (3)
Share w.c.	120 (62)	114 (69)
Sole use of w.c.	67 (34)	46 (27)
Total number from waiting list	193 (100)	165 (100)

Since Lambeth's housing programme concentrated on areas
of housing gain and there was a large demand for small dwellings from households in these areas, it is not surprising that the
GLC's redistributive role should be seen as the answer to the
problem created by the demand from families with children.
Of the sample of Lambeth nominees to the GLC, 35 per cent
were eventually rehoused in Outer London. Of these 41 per cent
had three or more children compared to 30 per cent of those
who remained in Inner London. In addition, other inner
boroughs may have relied on the GLC in the same way. Of the

---

already being Lambeth tenants when rehoused. In these cases the local
authority had compulsorily acquired the dwellings and the tenure prior
to the acquisition was not recorded. This hardly affected waiting list
cases but for clearance cases 57 per cent were recorded as already being
local authority tenants without any mention of previous tenure.

Table 1.3

Council Tenants Samples
Socio-economic Groups: Five Local Authority Samples (percentages)

	Employers, managers, and professionals	Non-manual workers	Foremen, skilled manual, and self-employed workers	Personal service workers, semi-skilled, and agricultural workers	Unskilled workers	Retired	Other (i.e. armed forces unemployed, no information)	Total
Lambeth tenants	4	12	29	15	10	19	11	100
Sutton tenants	3	14	33	16	9	10	15	100
Lambeth nominees to the GLC	4	13	33	16	11	11	12	100
GLC Southern District Office	3	14	26	10	6	25	17	100
GLC St Helier District Office	1	13	41	14	7	20	4	100

families rehoused in the St Helier District in Sutton 86 per cent were nominees from one inner borough or another.

So the best chance for households with children generally lay in Outer London. And the best way of getting there was by registering on a waiting list and getting nominated to the GLC. Of Lambeth's nominees to the GLC 63 per cent came from the waiting list and over 50 per cent of the London borough nominees who were rehoused by the GLC in the St Helier District in Sutton were from (Inner London) waiting lists. However, households in some of the worst conditions were not necessarily on waiting lists.

Table 1.4

Council Tenants Samples
Average Incomes of Tenants

Lambeth tenants (1970–71)	Lambeth nominees (1970–71)	Lambeth nominees rehoused in Inner London (1970–71)	Lambeth nominees rehoused in Outer London (1970–71)	Sutton tenants (1970–71)	Borough nominees to Sutton (1970–71)
£19.00	£20.50	£18.90	£23.45	£21.00	£23.00

The F test shows the differences to be significant at the 1 per cent level, i.e. the differences between these average incomes could only be expected to have occurred by chance less than one time in a hundred.

Because of this under-representation of households in worst conditions on the waiting list it is not surprising to find that the higher socio-economic groups had a better chance of being rehoused. The distributions in Table 1.3 conform to the general distribution of groups in the population rather than to the concentration of housing need among the lower groups in the areas of multiple occupation as portrayed, for example, by the Francis Committee [5]. There is a slightly higher proportion of the upper socio-economic groups in the Lambeth nominee and the St Helier samples. A more significant difference between the various samples however occurs for incomes.[39] Table 1.4

---

[39] The samples were taken over different time spans, but there were enough households in the Lambeth and Sutton tenant samples rehoused in 1970–71 to provide income figures which could be compared to those of the Lambeth nominees. Unfortunately this was not the case for other samples.

shows that the average head of household gross income was significantly higher for families who left for Outer London from Inner London. The difference can only partly be accounted for by the different proportions of tenants on low, fixed incomes from the state.[40]

Larger families, higher socio-economic groups, and higher earners were thus going to Outer London. Larger families who wanted a council house often had to move out of Lambeth because of the smaller size of dwellings currently being built in Lambeth. The higher income groups were probably more able to move because they could afford the increased fares to work that were likely to ensue. Conversely large *poor* families were less likely to move to Outer London but we do not know whether this pattern was the result of voluntary decisions or the selection processes of the receiving authorities.

What were the 'spatial' results of public housing policies in London? The redistribution of population was minimal with respect to the GLC's own development activities in Lambeth. Of the families which these activities displaced from the borough 94 per cent were rehoused in Inner London. Lambeth's nominations to the GLC however achieved a wider spread; only 65 per cent of families were rehoused in Inner London, the bulk of the other families were rehoused in the outer south London area, 18 per cent of all families going to Sutton and Merton alone. A distinct radial movement towards the south-west was evident in this sample and in the case of rehousing by the GLC on its St Helier estate in Sutton, which received 56 per cent of its new tenants from Lambeth, Southwark, and Wandsworth. (Apart from Hammersmith, no other borough contributed over 10 per cent of the families rehoused on the GLC St Helier estate.) Similarly, in the case of Sutton Borough Council's own estates, most of the nominees from Inner London came from Lambeth and the two adjacent boroughs of Wandsworth and Southwark, and some also from Hammersmith.

---

[40] In 1970–71 both Lambeth tenant and Lambeth nominee samples have the same percentages of low incomes from retired and unemployed people (22 per cent). For Sutton the figure was 16 per cent. For Lambeth nominees who remained in Inner London it was 23 per cent, and for those going to Outer London, 18 per cent.

The Limitations of a Comprehensive Housing Policy

In the Introduction we referred to various conceptions of a comprehensive housing policy. Both the GLC and Sutton, in the period we studied, favoured a 'co-operative' approach, relying heavily on the private sector.[41] In this situation the limits to what they did in the field of public housing were conterminous with the limits of what they were prepared to do. Thus the problem of land availability for public housing which faced all our three authorities was far less important in practice for Sutton and the GLC than for Lambeth.

The GLC was, however, in a somewhat more complex situation than Sutton for, although sharing that borough's general philosophy towards housing, it had some responsibility to help inner boroughs to meet their public housing needs under provisions in the 1963 London Government Act. It was also the case, in the period we studied, that Conservatives were in power in many Inner London boroughs (such as Lambeth) and they also wanted GLC help. The outcome of all these pressures was that the GLC did little more than continue the existing arrangements for the public sector that they inherited on taking power from Labour in 1967 and did not make any positive attempt to expand this role.

Lambeth on the other hand was faced with pressing problems which made it a practical impossibility to play as positive a role in public housing as the local Conservatives wanted. As we saw in the last section, land and staff shortage, the conflict between socio-economic and housing aims, and, to some extent, finance, all combined to limit the extent to which public housing could be provided within the borough to meet existing and future needs.

In this situation Lambeth had to look elsewhere for help—primarily towards the GLC and the outer boroughs. Our examination of Sutton's policies illustrates how and why the majority of outer boroughs were unwilling to give inner areas such as Lambeth the help they required. We have also seen that

---

[41] In the GLC's case this was possibly a more consciously adopted position than in Sutton because in the former case it was a reaction to the approach of their Labour predecessors whereas in the latter case there was a long tradition of placing a higher priority on the private sector.

the GLC while continuing to be of strategic importance in helping to meet the borough's public housing goals, was unwilling to expand its effort to the extent that the borough would have wished. Therefore in Lambeth, unlike Sutton or the GLC, the approach to a comprehensive housing policy was mainly limited by constraints rather than ideology.[42] In the long run as well, the effect of the housing programme on the rates might have become an issue whose political repercussions limited the programme but this did not happen during the period we reviewed. In fact the Lambeth Conservatives used this possibility in order to put pressure on the national government to alter the subsidy system so that it would give inner areas more help. The 1972 Housing Finance Act did this.[43] However this measure did not in any way ease the land availability problem. The need for help from other areas and authorities remained the major obstacle to achieving the public-sector goals of Lambeth's comprehensive housing policy.

References

1. *Into the Seventies: A Review of Demand, Supply, and Costs.* London Borough of Lambeth, 1970.

2. CULLINGWORTH, J. B. *Report to the Minister of Housing and Local Government on the Proposals for Transfer of GLC Housing to the London Boroughs* (2 volumes) (London: H.M.S.O., 1970).

3. NEVITT, D. and RHODES, G. in 'Housing', Chapter 7 of *The New Government of London: The First Five Years*, G. Rhodes (editor) (London: Weidenfeld and Nicolson, 1972).

4. *Housing Statistics Part 1* (London: Institute of Municipal Treasurers and Accountants, 1971).

5. FRANCIS COMMITTEE. *Report of the Committee on the Rent Acts*, Cmnd 4609 (London: H.M.S.O., 1971), Appendix 1, pp. 241–316.

---

[42] Except to the extent that the attempt to provide 25 per cent of new housing from private sources was a goal. This was largely abandoned anyway as its impracticability became evident.

[43] This issue may recur however. At the start of 1972 the Borough Treasurer estimated that the new subsidy system would cut the then current annual deficit of £2m on the housing revenue account by 50 per cent. However by 1974, it was expected to be up to £2m again.

Chapter Two

Local Authorities: House Purchase

Background

Local authorities have been encouraged not only to build houses for renting but also to lend money for house purchase. A series of Small Dwelling Acquisition Acts dating from the nineteenth century has enabled local authorities to lend money and the two major acts which consolidated and extended their powers in this field are the Housing (Financial Provisions) Act 1958, and the House Purchase and Housing Act 1959. For several years after these Acts were passed, councils were given very little guidance by the Ministry about the amount of money they should lend for house purchase or the categories of persons to whom they should lend. In 1965, a Ministerial circular asked for information about whom local authorities were giving mortgages to and in 1971 authorities were asked to limit their lending to 'categories of borrowers who might not qualify for a building society loan or who are otherwise in need'. [1] Some of the principal categories that the Minister was concerned with were—

1 Homeless people.
2 People living in overcrowded conditions, or conditions otherwise detrimental to health.
3 People displaced by slum-clearance or other development.
4 People who want to buy old and smaller homes unlikely to attract a commercial mortgage advance.
5 People high on the authority's waiting list.
6 Existing tenants of the local authority.

There is thus a clear expectation that local authority mortgage schemes should go some way at least to providing an alternative to people who would normally look to the local authority's own housing stock for help. There is hope that local authorities will to some extent play a role in a comprehensive lending policy as 'lenders of last resort'. Let us examine the aims of the schemes run by our three local authorities and the constraints facing their operations and see to what extent local authority mortgage schemes come anywhere near playing a meaningful role in a comprehensive housing strategy at local, and central government level.

The Aims of the Local Authority Mortgage Schemes

The lack of explicit guidance by central government until recently has meant that the local authorities have been free to develop their schemes as their ideology allowed. Lambeth as we have seen has had extreme difficulty in finding enough land for building. Its mortgage scheme was therefore made available to people who lived in the borough but who wanted to move out and buy elsewhere. The scheme was intended to be an important part of the general approach of the Housing Advice Centre which asked people coming in for help, 'do you need to continue living in Lambeth?' However people from outside Lambeth could also use the scheme to buy in the borough and insufficient attention was given to helping poorer families. Until 1970 the mortgage allowed was based solely on the head of household's income, and the wife's income was ignored. The preoccupation with the Advice Centre's approach of getting people out of Lambeth probably led to this situation.

The GLC's scheme in contrast was for several years aimed at helping people who fell within a number of tightly defined categories. They would lend to their own tenants, to people who were homeless, overcrowded, or living in unhealthy conditions, to tenants of properties blighted by near-by development which a building society would not consider, to people dislodged by GLC projects, to people who were moving to new or expanding towns and to people who had been tenants of housing associations for more than two years. The GLC was ideologically disposed towards promoting owner occupation[1] and their scheme was a conscious attempt to be 'a lender of last resort'.[2] More recently the council became far less restrictive as it had acquired more money for lending. The scheme had at all times been open to residents of Greater London who want to buy anywhere in England and Wales but in general it was deliberately aimed at helping the marginal buyer (taking into account the regular income of other members of the family) who wanted to buy older property. In fact the GLC was often accused of over-committing people who are then forced to default should they become unemployed or get into other difficulties. The scheme has also been accused of contributing to multiple occupation because of its tendency to over-commit people since mortgagors will take in lodgers to help with the mortgage repayments. This shows the difficulty of fulfilling the role of lender of last resort particularly in Inner London but it highlights quite clearly the GLC's aim of helping the marginal buyer.

Sutton, for a number of reasons, had the most liberal scheme of the three. They had the most generous earnings rule (lending three as opposed to two and a half times annual income, including wife's income in many cases) and the lowest interest rate (using the pool rate of interest[3] of the authority's consolidated loan fund). Unlike the Lambeth and GLC schemes, Sutton's scheme was restricted to lending on pre-1919 houses within the borough. But like the GLC's scheme it was deliberately aimed at helping marginal buyers wanting to purchase older property and in addition it had an 'accelerated repayment' position for young marrieds.[4] In many ways both the GLC and Sutton schemes showed a willingness on the part of

---

[1] Unlike some councils. In 1968 Tower Hamlets for instance only made eight loans for house purchase. It seems unlikely that this represents the true potential for this facility in that borough. See Ministry of Housing and Local Government, *Local Housing Statistics No. 7*, August 1968, London: H.M.S.O.

[2] GLC, Minutes, 23 March, 1971, p. 175. 'The Council is thus a lender of last resort.'

[3] This is the average rate of interest which the authority pays on all the money it borrows for whatever purpose. It therefore contains a concealed subsidy from the rates.

[4] Whereby more of the mortgage was paid off than usual in the early years before they have children and the wife has to stop work.

the two local authorities to subsidize people to an extent which would never be countenanced in their policies towards council tenants.

The Problems They Faced

The main problems are threefold. Firstly, there is the policy of central government in advancing the money to local authorities. Secondly, there is the problem of staffing. And thirdly, there is the problem of the internal organization of mortgage lending within the local authority. Rising home prices are also a constraint facing any scheme aimed at the marginal buyer but, as we shall see, these are related to the first main problem—the policies of central government.

Central government has lent local authorities money for mortgages in accordance with national economic policy. When there are restrictions on public spending it has reduced the amount of money it is prepared to see local authorities advancing for house purchase. As a result there has been a series of alternate relaxations and restrictions on the amount of money made available for these purposes. Table 2.1 shows how the local authority sector has fluctuated in comparison with the relatively steady growth of building society and insurance company lending.

Table 2.1

Advances for House Purchase: Main institutional sources,
UK, £ million

Year	Building societies	Local authorities	Insurance companies
1960	558	78	—
1961	544	107	—
1962	618	94	118
1963	852	119	107
1964	1052	195	132
1965	965	244	163
1966	1245	134	147
1967	1477	167	124
1968	1587	108	168
1969	1556	70	179
1970	2021	154	154

Source: Department of the Environment, *Housing Statistics No. 23*, November 1971.

Restrictions create severe problems for the local authorities, apart from making them unable to lend as much money as they would like. It is useless setting up the staff and organization to process £30m worth of mortgages a year if at very short notice only £5m is then available. Yet this happened to the GLC between 1967 and 1969. Lambeth had the same problem in reverse in 1969–70 when the quota was expected to be £392 000, was suddenly cut to £85 600 and then near the end of the year increased to £374 500. Apart from the fact that many would-be buyers at the start of the year had had to be refused and had lost interest in the properties, the radically escalating staff requirements meant that it proved impossible to use all the quota by the end of the financial year. In 1970–71 only about 60 per cent of the available money was spent.

These difficulties have given rise to the second main problem, that of staff shortage. Since it is useless to employ all the staff needed to deal with a peak supply of money, heavy reliance has been placed on the services of outside valuers by all our three local authorities at times of high demand for mortgages. For example, the GLC quota rose from £5m in 1968–69 to £50m in 1970–71, and in that year some 30 per cent of the valuation work had to be done by outside firms. Even when outsiders are brought in, the strain on the core organization can be such that mortgage approval takes an inordinate time and the house is lost. These complaints have been frequent concerning the GLC scheme in particular. Some estate agents advised vendors to have nothing to do with would be purchasers who said that they require a GLC loan. It is also the case that outside valuers have tended to apply overstringent and some-times even irrelevant criteria. They are used to valuing for building societies and are often far more critical of older property than is warranted, being either unable or unwilling to recognize that the local authorities are prepared to take a more generous and probably more realistic view of the security of a house than the societies.

There are several cases in our sample where Lambeth actually loaned more than the surveyor's valuation on a property because of this attitude but in many cases they accepted what might well have been an overstringent valu-ation. Sutton also told us that the outside valuers they used had been reducing their valuations in an unjustifiable way because of such minor faults in the property as settlement cracks or because of rather subjective assessments such as that, for example, certain properties might be difficult to resell. Sutton has specifically instructed their valuers to cease these practices.

In 1971 Sutton finally resolved the two problems of (a) having to dismiss or redeploy staff when there were restrictions on its lending quota and (b) having to use the services of the unduly restrictive valuation profession when it could lend more than it had planned for, by restricting the amount it was prepared to lend to £1m a year, despite the fact that it was allowed by central government to lend more than this.

By 1972 there was no central government restriction on local authority mortgage lending. This might be beneficial for housing policy but there are several drawbacks.

Firstly, although this policy fits in well with government's wish to encourage owner occupation, it also fits in well with a need to expand economic activity by increasing government spending. In other words it is still largely a product of the requirements of national economic policy rather than housing policy and the amount available to lend is still liable to be cut back at any time, thus creating the sort of organizational problems referred to above and causing a sharp decline in the chances for owner occupation for many people on moderate incomes.

Secondly, in London there is a shortage of suitable housing and the sudden injection of a great deal of money from local authorities and from building societies too drives prices up rapidly. Some argue that this is merely restoring the balance between house prices and incomes that existed formerly.[5] But

---

[5] See, for example, *The Sunday Times*, Colour Supplement, 16 April, 1972. An article by the paper's Insight Consumer Unit on inflation of house prices argues that rises in earnings and house prices have usually kept step. However the 'most savage credit squeeze in years' beginning in 1968 depressed house prices while earnings continued to rise. The argument is that the rapid rise in prices in 1971–72 is merely a catching up process. As an explanation of national trends this argument may be valid but—as the article admits—the very fast increases in price in areas such as London are likely to be due to severe scarcity which is not going to be quickly eased. Even if many new houses were built the addition to the stock would only be marginal. There must also be some doubt concerning whether the incomes of the lower-paid workers who are marginal house-buyers have in fact kept up with the overall increase in incomes.

it is clear that in a situation where house prices are probably inflating faster than incomes it is doubtful whether there is any overall benefit to the marginal buyer from this increased availability of funds.

The third constraint we want to discuss reflects the position of the housing department within each local authority. As far as Lambeth's housing department was concerned the organization of mortgage approval was a constraint. So far as the other two housing departments were concerned it was not, because housing policy did not emanate from a powerful housing department but from elsewhere in the council.

In all three authorities the administration of the mortgage schemes was not a part of the activities of the housing departments. Policies were generated and the schemes run from the Treasurer's Departments. It is not surprising that these schemes should be run by the Treasurer's Department in the GLC and Sutton as neither of them has attempted to mount an integrated attack on housing problems within their areas. However, the separation of functions in Lambeth was surprising and though the mortgage scheme was run as a part of the Directorate of Housing and Property Services from the Housing Advice Centre, it was still partly controlled by the Treasurer as we mentioned in Chapter One. This partly accounted for the resistance from officers when the Conservatives—having liberalized the scheme in 1970—wished to make further amendments to it. The scheme was left alone when all other aspects of housing were being reorganized and redirected in Lambeth and the Housing Department and the politicians assumed that it would operate in accordance with the overall housing ideology.

Let us now examine the effects of all these ideologies and constraints.

Who got Council Mortgages?

The effects of the different schemes of the authorities clearly show in the data we collected.[6]

The figures in Table 2.2 support the contention made above,

---

[6] See the Appendix for details of the samples.

Table 2.2

Local Authority Mortgage Samples
Sutton, Lambeth, and GLC Mortgages 1965–71

	GLC	Lambeth	Sutton
Mean price of house	£4762	£5694	£4516
Median annual income of main and secondary borrower (if applicable)	£1609	£1869	£1496
Percentage with 100 per cent mortgages	65%	7%	38%
Percentage with a term of twenty-five years or over	94%	31%	70%
Occupations			
(a) skilled and semi-skilled manual workers	55%	43%	42%
(b) managerial professionals and other white collar workers	30%	38%	46%

that the Lambeth scheme was less attractive to marginal buyers than either the Sutton or GLC ones. The average prices of the houses bought under all three schemes were similar and so the higher income requirement in Lambeth could only have been a product of more stringent rules. Comparison of the percentage gaining 100 per cent mortgages and long terms in Lambeth with those in Sutton and for the GLC underlines this. Furthermore 23 per cent of all mortgagors in Lambeth were granted a shorter term than they had initially requested.

The age distribution of mortgagors also highlights the distinction between the GLC and Sutton schemes on the one hand and the Lambeth scheme on the other. Almost half the Sutton and GLC mortgagors were under thirty whereas only just over one-quarter of the Lambeth mortgagors were. Also only 7 per cent of Lambeth borrowers were under twenty-five whereas 24 per cent of GLC buyers and 28 per cent of Sutton buyers were in this group. A great number of these borrowers would have been young families who were likely to need special help in order to buy.

Examination of the data, showed that all three schemes catered mainly for two groups, skilled and semi-skilled manual workers and white-collar workers. Unskilled manual workers on the whole did not benefit except from the GLC scheme in its early years. However the effects of Sutton's generous earning rule were evident for over 80 per cent of its skilled and semi-skilled workers and over 70 per cent of its white-collar workers

earned under £35 per week, compared to under 50 per cent of
each group in the other two schemes.

Lambeth's scheme showed its essential limitation when
we considered whether applicants got less money than they
initially wanted because their property was valued at less than
the purchase price, or whether they received less than they
wanted because they did not fulfil the income requirements.
Line 1 of Table 2.3 is an overall measure of the percentages of
those who received less than they asked for. It shows that the
GLC failed to satisfy most often and Sutton least but that in all
three authorities substantial numbers of borrowers received less

Table 2.3

Local Authority Mortgage Samples
Sutton, Lambeth, and GLC Mortgages 1965–71. Relationships between
valuation and advances required and received

	GLC %	Lambeth %	Sutton %
1. Advance granted less than advance required	45	32	23
2. Valuation less than advance required	44	7	15
3. Advance granted less than advance required but advance required not greater than valuation	2	23	8

than they required. Lines 2 and 3 break down 1 according to
whether the loan was reduced for reasons of the valuation of
the property (line 2) or income of applicant (line 3). Two
features are prominent here, the first is that almost all the GLC
loans that were lower than requested were because properties
were valued below the loan required, perhaps because they
relied on outside valuers more than the other two schemes. The
second feature is that almost a quarter of Lambeth's loans were
less than required because of insufficient income. This means
that a larger number of Lambeth than GLC or Sutton mortgagors had to find money elsewhere—probably at higher cost—
because of the rather stringent rules of Lambeth's scheme (at
least until 1970).

Lambeth's scheme was doubly disappointing. Not only did
it fail to extend house purchase to marginal buyers but it also
failed to be taken up by Lambeth residents who wanted

to move outside the Borough. Only 10 per cent of our sample bought property outside Lambeth. However, this figure is increasing as the Housing Advice Centre has time to have more effect. By 1972 the proportion was reported to be approaching a third of all borrowers—although there was no indication that poorer people were benefiting from this. Fortunately for Lambeth very few people in our sample came from outside the borough to counter the small flow of people moving out to buy via its scheme.

The GLC and Sutton schemes were far more successful in redistributing population although they had no explicit goal for doing so. Almost a half of the GLC mortgagors originated in Inner London and 60 per cent of these moved to Outer London or beyond. But again there was no evidence that those who moved to Outer London via the GLC scheme had incomes which differed materially from those who stayed in Inner London. And with more people moving to Outer London and beyond the GLC scheme was far less successful in getting people to buy older (pre-1919) property than the other two schemes: 42 per cent of the houses it lent money on were of this age, while Lambeth and Sutton's proportions were 68 per cent and 60 per cent respectively—Lambeth because of its Inner London location and Sutton because its scheme was aimed specifically at such property.

Sutton also managed to attract 40 per cent of its mortgagors from outside its borough boundaries but only a third of these were from Inner London. The other two-thirds came equally from the rest of Outer London and from outside Greater London altogether. But Sutton lent £4m as opposed to Lambeth's £2.9m from 1965 to 1971 (approximate sums). It was unintentionally doing more to fulfil Lambeth's goal of getting prospective house purchasers to move out of Inner London (though not specifically from Lambeth) than Lambeth itself was over these years.

The GLC scheme did show that a local authority was capable of lending money to people who were tenants. 56 per cent of loans went to people from the unfurnished rented sector, 22 per cent to people from the furnished rented sector, and 20 per cent to council tenants. However, as we have noted, its mortgagors were not among the lowest income groups. The Sutton scheme was more successful in this respect, but neither

Sutton nor Lambeth kept data on the previous tenure of their borrowers.

But regardless of how one scheme was better than another, the rise in house prices in London generally in 1971–72 could have affected marginal buyers far more than any individual differences in earnings rules or whatever. The data we collected is unfortunately quite inadequate to test this assertion for these years. But the 1970–71 data for the GLC[7] in Table 2.4

Table 2.4

GLC Mortgage Sample
Incomes and House Prices 1965–67 and 1970–71. GLC Scheme

Year	Percentage of borrowers with combined incomes of less than £35 per week	Percentage of houses priced at £5000 or more
1965	75	30
1966	79	25
1967	76	24
1970	12	51
1971	9	54

Note: Numbers were too small in 1968–69 to be significant.

shows quite clearly that the effects of the injection of large amounts of money, by building societies as well as local authorities were being felt by marginal buyers before the main 'boom' in house prices in 1972.

By 1970 the average price of houses with GLC mortgages was still, at £5021 (£5144 in 1971), about £1700–£2500 cheaper than the average price of homes which gained a building society mortgage. So it could still be claimed that, despite rapidly worsening conditions for local authority borrowers in 1970–71, these schemes still served a different and poorer market than that of the building societies. Let us now take up this point and discuss to what extent the local authorities were able and willing to play a part in a comprehensive house purchase system where they could act as 'lenders of last resort'.

[7] We cannot compare the Lambeth and Sutton data because the figures in our samples for these years were too small.

The Limitations of a Comprehensive Housing Policy

We can see from the GLC data that local authorities do help a large number of people to own their own homes for the first time. However the extent to which their schemes appear effective in acting as a 'lender of last resort' varies. Somewhat surprisingly, of the three authorities we looked at, Lambeth was the least successful in this respect.

Various factors determine whom the local authority schemes serve. Some are more generous than others, depending partly on whether the politicians want to encourage owner occupation and partly on the attitudes of officers as to how stringent the rules of the scheme should be. However, despite this, a major constraint in the operation of all local authority schemes has been the policy of central government of restricting and releasing funds in accordance with economic rather than housing considerations.

However, the local authority schemes may nevertheless be acting as 'lenders of last resort', since they remain more generous than building societies (as will be shown in Chapter Four), even in a situation where they may be able to offer their generosity to fewer and fewer people as house prices increase. In actual fact there is no doubt that because of the constraints facing council mortgage schemes and the ideology of some of them, they are not the 'lenders of last resort'.

It seems clear from our own sources and from evidence given to the House of Commons Select Committee on Race Relations (in Lambeth, Lewisham, and Paddington) that finance companies (mainly merchant banks) perform this role.[8] We have no reliable indication of the size of their involvement in financing owner occupation in London but the terms they offer tend to be so much worse than those of the local authorities or building societies that we would expect these agencies' operations to be concentrated in areas where the ability to qualify for other loans is least, i.e. in the stress areas.

The companies are not concerned with the social implications

---

[8] See, for example, *Minutes of Evidence*, The Select Committee on Race Relations and Immigration; 4 February, 1971, evidence of Mr Simon Hillyard (Lambeth); 1 March, 1971, evidence of the Lewisham Citizen's Advice Bureau; 2 March, 1971, evidence of the City of Westminster.

of what they are doing. They are simply providing a financial service and are not usually agencies specializing in housing loans unlike the building societies. Nor are they governed by a law which recognizes some special significance in their role, nor controlled by the government in any direct way nor, apparently, are they particularly concerned with maintaining a public image of social responsibility. They seem to be willing to lend to anyone who can meet their terms and regard defaulters simply as bad debtors. Like any other commercial concern, they take fairly prompt action to recover their property in such circumstances. Unlike the societies they do not have a steady flow of investors who are prepared to accept relatively low-interest rates. They have to borrow at the commercial rate and lend at an even higher rate.

Lawyers themselves have the greatest difficulty in understanding how much legal protection the borrower has but cases we have seen suggest that it is minimal when compared with building society mortgages or even HP contracts. The concealment from the borrower of the true rate of interest he will pay on loans is quite normal. The situation is one where the crudest form of exploitation is easily practised.

We have been told that these company schemes fall into two categories. The first type charges 15–16 per cent interest on the reducing principal. This is a fairly reasonable form of agreement given the high rate of interest which these companies pay for money. The second type advertise lower rates, say 10–12 per cent to attract custom, but do not reduce the principal during the term of the loan so that the true interest rate may be about 30 per cent. It seems that this is not often explained to the borrower. All loans tend to be over a short period, 5–15 years is common, so that repayments are high. The consequences of this situation for the privately rented sector are discussed in Chapter Five.

A number of people working in the housing field have collected details of these mortgages and some interesting aspects emerge:

1 Some companies run schemes where intending buyers have to pay off a large deposit, say £1000 on a £6000 house, before being granted a mortgage. The deposit is paid off by them over a number of years. At the same time, they

are already paying interest on the amount of the loan which will, at the end of this period, be lent to them. Meanwhile the clients occupy the house as licencees without any of the statutory protection of other types of tenancy.

2 The agreements are often so difficult to interpret that even the courts do not understand them. One lawyer suggested to us that if they did they would often not agree to give judgement in favour of these companies for repossession.

3 On foreclosure the companies are only supposed to take from the buyers the money still owing to them. However there seems to be no control on the amount they add to the amount actually owed as fees for selling, cost of foreclosure, etc. Often the buyer finds that, despite the fact that he has paid out a great deal of money, there is nothing left for him.

4 Many estate agents, mortgage brokers, and solicitors act as agents for these loans without making it clear to the borrower that they are not normal building society mortgages.

As we have said these loans are particularly common in stress areas. Direct evidence is hard to obtain but one recent newspaper article claimed that 70 per cent of the mortgages given by one of the most prominent local estate agents in Lambeth were arranged through finance companies.[9] It is particularly difficult to avoid attributing this high figure to the operations of Lambeth's scheme and the constraints facing it. For Lambeth, like other authorities, is faced with the 'booms and slumps' of mortgage financing from central government. This leads to reliance on outside valuers when money is plentiful because of the difficulties in recruiting extra staff at short notice. This in turn leads to a more restrictive valuation of properties which means that purchasers have to find large amounts of money to finance the gap between the valuation and purchase price. On top of all this an over-cautious earnings rule will add to the difficulties people face in getting a mortgage in

---

[9] This is confirmed by our examination of the register of multiple occupation, see Chapter Five.

the first place. As a result a different 'lender of last resort' has emerged.

By 1973 the government announced that it intended to curb 'the growing abuses of the £300 million a year second mortgage market'.[10] It proposed a voluntary code whereby companies will be asked among other things to disclose the true rate of interest of their loans. These steps were seen as a stop gap to meet public criticism until the proposed Consumer Credit Bill, for which no date has been fixed, is published.

The problem remains that even if the abuses are stopped completely, the demand for a 'lender of last resort' will still remain. The limitations in what the government would like to see the local authorities doing has led to the finance companies filling the role. Controls on finance companies will not significantly affect the constraints facing people since these arise from the ideology behind local authority schemes and, more importantly, the constraints affecting them.

The only conclusion can be that central government has not yet allowed local authorities to come anywhere near fulfilling the role expected of them, despite the willingness of authorities to promote owner occupation by being in some cases far more sympathetic towards this form of public enterprise than they would ever be towards public housing generally.

Let us now see how the various comprehensive policies have fared in their intervention in the private sector.

Reference

1. *Local Authority Advances for House Purchase.* Circular 22/71. Department of the Environment, London: March 1971.

---

[10] Report in *The Guardian*, 20 February, 1973.

PART TWO

Private Enterprise and Public Intervention

Chapter Three

Housing Associations

Background

A growing lobby in the 1960s expressed anxiety at what they saw as the increasing municipalization of the housing market in British towns. They stressed the necessity for a 'third arm' to replace the fading functions of the private landlord and to provide an alternative to local authority housing to rent. This lobby included Conservatives, who had always argued for an increased role for private enterprise in the provision of housing, and the Labour Party, who—as we mentioned in the Introduction—had dropped the idea of municipalization of the privately rented sector from their programme at the end of the 1950s. The objective of increasing philanthropic contributions towards the cost of providing housing fitted in with the governmental need to reduce public expenditure. The increasing emphasis in the 1960s on rehabilitation rather than redevelopment in housing policy gave housing associations a more clearly defined role.

Some housing associations date from nineteenth-century attempts to provide charitable help for the poor. A lot more sprang up in the sixties in response to the government's increased emphasis on the contribution that the associations might make and the extra powers that local authorities were given to help them. In London, especially with the coming to power of the Conservatives in many boroughs, there was a rapid increase in the number of associations and the dwellings they provided.[1] The housing association dwellings were often

---

[1] In 1967 the number of dwellings provided by housing associations in

considered by the Conservatives as an alternative to further 'soulless' council blocks. Many Labour-controlled boroughs have however continued to support the associations because of the additional help and resources it was felt they could bring to the relief of housing problems.

This political ambiguity in the reasons for the encouragement of housing associations has been reflected in their activities. As a result it has never been clear whether they should be housing those in need who would normally look to the local authority, or housing those categories such as the single, students or the homeless, whom a pressurized local authority with a long waiting list could not hope to cater for.[2]

By 1970 their contribution was declining because of the constraints they faced.[3] Although the associations were publicly and charitably subsidized they were still subject to market forces, to particular conditions attached to the subsidies they obtained, and to particular organizational constraints. Together these factors determined to what extent a socially-oriented 'charitable ethic', whether aimed at providing an alternative or a supplement to the local authority's role, could contribute towards a comprehensive housing policy.

The Aims of the Housing Associations

We looked in detail at the operations of two associations in Lambeth, the London Housing Trust (LHT) and the Metropolitan Housing Trust (MHT). Both of these were supported by the Lambeth Council. We chose also to look at one association backed by the GLC, the Family Housing Association (FHA), which received a large proportion of the GLC allo-

---

London operating with support from the boroughs and GLC was 469; in 1968 it was 739; and in 1969 it was 1797. (Authors communication with D.O.E.)

[2] For example the Ministry Circular 73/67 stressed that the subsidy for associations to acquire and convert under the 1967 Housing Subsidies Act was particularly intended to encourage the work of those associations meeting the needs of families who were homeless or living in bad or over-crowded conditions leading to homelessness.

[3] The 1969 figure of 1797 dwellings completed fell to 1082 in 1970.

cation to housing associations and was active in the area of South London with which we were concerned.[4]

All these associations had similar aims to the extent that they were 'general need' associations. In other words, like local authorities they were attempting to house families who were living in poor conditions. On the other hand the associations were motivated to a greater or lesser extent by the feeling, generally held in the housing association movement, that local authorities missed out crucial sectors of need, such as unskilled workers, households with large families, or those in danger of becoming homeless. We shall examine to what extent our associations were doing one or other of these two things, to what extent they helped out by reinforcing the local authorities' housing functions, and to what extent they added to the range of needs met by the local authorities.

The aims of the two associations we examined in Sutton differed radically from those mentioned above. Before the rapid expansion of associations in the sixties, which was linked to the supposed contribution they could make to the relief of hard-core housing need in inner city areas, associations had traditionally catered for a range of minority needs such as the aged and the handicapped. In Sutton, where Lambeth-style housing stress was virtually non-existent, most of the associations fell into this traditional pattern and many, encouraged by the council, specialized in housing old people. This was the case for our two associations, the Castlemead Housing Association (CHA) and the Sutton Housing Society (SHS), which were the two largest ones operating in the borough.[5]

One further difference between the two groups of associations needs to be noted. The inner area, general needs associations mainly aimed at converting existing properties—inevitable in

---

[4] By 1971 the London Housing Trust had acquired, converted and let 79 properties in Lambeth, comprising 170 dwelling units. The Metropolitan had purchased 40 properties which were being converted into 84 units. Thirty-two had been let by 1971. FHA owned 157 units in Lambeth by 1971, all of which had been acquired and converted with GLC assistance. In addition the GLC had made available 33 units of short-life property which they owned, for FHA to let on a temporary basis.

[5] By 1971 the CHA had eight schemes in progress or completed, all of which were conversions. By 1971 the SHS had 76 units completed and 65 in the process of being built, located on five sites in the borough.

an area of very high costs and limited land availability. In Sutton, where these factors were less of a constraint, new building was far more common. Although the CHA had done some conversions, the SHS was solely concerned with new building.

Let us see to what extent their goals were affected by the problems faced in the two different areas.

Their Operations and Constraints

The associations were constrained by their relationship with the local authority in whose area they wanted to work, by the availability of finance and the conditions attached to it, and by the availability of land and housing.

Housing associations have a status defined in legislation by central government[6] but like other housing agencies, they are controlled by various processes of accountability. Local authorities have permissive powers to support housing associations but are not obliged to and associations are thus dependent on the local authority's interpretation of the role they should play. When many local authorities came under Conservative control in 1968, the councils often saw the existence of housing associations as a way of implementing a Conservative housing policy despite the restrictions on rents which the then Ministry of Housing and Local Government was attempting to impose on local authorities through the Prices and Incomes Board.

However the Lambeth, Sutton, and GLC associations were not constrained very much by the local authority's interpretation of the role they should play. In Lambeth and the GLC they were given a very broad brief to help the local authorities generally, although we shall have more to say about the GLC's motives later. In Sutton the associations were encouraged to

---

[6] S.119, 120, 121 of Housing Act 1957.
S.12 of Housing Subsidies Act 1967.
S.21 of Housing Act 1969.
The 1957 Housing Act empowered local authorities to pass on Exchequer Subsidy to housing associations for new building and acquisition and conversion, and to make a rate fund contribution. The 1967 and 1969 Housing Acts increased the subsidy available to three-eighths of the annual loan charges on the costs of acquisition and conversion up to a maximum of £2500 per dwelling in Greater London.

provide for specific needs, such as the elderly, which the council thought the public sector should be concentrating on. But in Sutton the local authority was also concerned about the proportion of council dwellings in the total stock. So it tended to concentrate on those associations who would provide for the groups it would otherwise have to provide for itself—the elderly and the physically handicapped. This was no constraint however on the 'specialist' associations concerned but it did mean that more 'generalist' associations might not have received such active support.

Shortage of funds is one of the most significant constraints on the activity of the newly established housing associations. Local authorities are able to make a rate fund contribution to housing associations but in most cases this is made conditional on the association granting up to 50 per cent nomination rights to the local authority. Agreements have to be made between housing associations and individual boroughs, with the result that different agreements may pertain to the same association's schemes in different boroughs. Also, up until the 1972 Housing Finance Act, where local authorities nominated a percentage of tenants they usually only rebated the rents of their own nominees so that anomalies arose where tenants of similar means living in the same housing association scheme paid different rents for the same accommodation.

In London, housing associations wishing to house any category of the 'needy' are dependent on the rate fund contribution to bring rents down from an economic rent level to anything resembling current 'fair rent' levels.[7] Rents and subsidy cannot generally be pooled even within the schemes produced by a housing association in one borough,[8] so that a surplus from one scheme cannot be used to reduce rent levels

---

[7] For example, in Lambeth, where 'fair rents' are charged, only two properties purchased by housing associations did not need rate fund subsidy to bridge the deficit between cost rents and fair rent levels.

[8] The situation is very confusing regarding this point. According to circular 64/69, housing associations can pool rents and subsidies in a GIA. The Ministry also told borough councils informally that pooling in a zoned area was permissible, but retracted this later, maintaining it was in fact illegal. Elsewhere, for individual purchasers, pooling has not been permitted.

on other schemes. While housing associations are non-profit-making organizations they cannot usually afford to run at a loss and the degree of local authority assistance will contribute towards determining the social characteristics of the clientele the associations house. By 1970, for example, the London Housing Trust was running at a deficit of £10 000 on twelve properties in Newham where the borough council made no rate fund contribution. The LHT was compelled to cease purchasing houses in Newham since they were having to let the tenancies at below cost rent owing to the difficulty they had experienced in finding tenants willing to pay rents which were substantially higher than council rents, without the opportunity of rebates.[9]

For some associations charitable funds have eased this predicament, but not all housing associations are able to obtain charitable support. LHT, for example, received £27 000 from the Rowntree Trust and £24 000 from the City Parochial Trust. Other associations such as Family Housing Association have received money from Shelter. But the ideologies of the different housing associations will determine whether and where they appeal for charity. For example, the LHT Management Committee asked the Max Rayne Foundation for support but persistently refused to ask Shelter for assistance even though Shelter actually offered LHT money to help them reduce their rents. LHT disliked what they saw as the 'political' image of Shelter.

Shortage of funds, however, can actually prevent those housing associations which want to house low-income families from being able to do so. Because housing associations cannot run at a loss they refrain from housing 'problem families' both because they do not want to run up rent arrears and because they do not have the resources to employ a social work supportive staff. Once their waiting list lengthens and housing associations realize they can only house a fraction of their

---

[9] Similar problems were encountered by LHT in Haringey. There the borough council paid no rate fund contribution but agreed to extend their rebate scheme to all LHT tenants on the agreement that cost rents would be charged. One of the main difficulties LHT had was to find tenants who could afford a £6 net rent for two-bedroomed flats, the borough council did not consider anyone earning over £20 per week as eligible and up till 1971 no tenants of LHT had yet qualified as eligible.

applicants, they can choose those tenants who they know will be able to meet the rent and not be a source of trouble.

This happened particularly with the Lambeth-based associations. Before Lambeth council agreed to extend its rebate scheme to all LHT tenants, the Trust refused applicants whom they considered would not be able to afford the rent.[10] Even subsequently, the Trust has turned down applications from people whom they consider might prove a source of trouble.[11]

The position with FHA was less clear cut. Although they charged 'fair rents' and usually chose those who could afford to pay the rent, they tried never to turn away fatherless families (who had been their sole clientele before 1970). In this case, as three-quarters of the mothers were on social security, the Supplementary Benefits Commission looked after the rent. Resort was also made to a number of charitable funds to aid hardship cases. FHA was also able to employ a welfare officer, paid for by Shelter.

In Sutton the financial problems were not so important. Catering exclusively for old people on pensions and Supplementary Benefit meant that the associations avoided the problems of insufficient means to pay high rents. They were thus less likely to be deflected from their aims of helping the needy than the Lambeth associations.[12]

---

[10] For example, in 1969 an African paintsprayer and his wife who was a nurse were refused a flat for themselves and their two children by the Trust because the Trust did not think they could afford the rent of £7.75.

[11] An application by an English couple (dustman and waitress) with two children was turned down because they had 'slatternly habits'.

In August 1970 an unmarried mother with four children, who was on probation, was refused accommodation by LHT, because the Trust did not think they could give her the necessary attention. She had been referred to the Trust by Tulse Hill Welfare Centre and also by Lambeth Children's Department because she had been living in one room, which the landlord now wanted for his own use.

[12] SHS built only for elderly people and all but one of the CHA schemes were also for the elderly. Their one other scheme was for young couples. The association let the properties to them for a three-year period during which a proportion of the rent was saved with a building society as a deposit for house purchase. However, owing to the fact that CHA forgot to apply to the council for the acquisition and conversion subsidy, the rents they charged were rather high and the original intention of helping lower-income families was not fulfilled.

Because of financial pressures housing associations in Inner London tend to convert houses in the way which offered optimum financial advantages to themselves, rather than relating the size of the converted units to the needs of those on their waiting lists. Exchequer subsidy was allocated per dwelling, and so associations tend to convert houses into as many smaller units as possible. The majority of housing association conversions were into two or fewer bedroom units[13] yet in most cases more than half the applications on their waiting list wanted three bedrooms or more. In Outer London this was not a problem since the Sutton associations were housing elderly tenants who required small units.

In addition to shortage of funds, housing associations also suffer diseconomies of scale. After it has acquired a few properties, a full-time salaried staff becomes essential for a housing association yet at that stage the costs of employing an administrative staff cannot easily be borne. In order to support this cost, more houses have to be acquired and converted so that more income can be obtained from subsidy and rents to offset against this expenditure. Housing associations thus quickly get caught up in the need to expand in order to remain financially stable. By December 1969, for example, Family Housing Association had 545 converted dwelling units but the annual salary and expense allowance of permanent administrative staff (excluding architects and legal fees) amounted to £15 000 and the total gross cost of administration, £25 000.[14] On the other hand Quadrant Housing Association owned 600 units at the end of 1969 (including those undergoing conversion) and

---

[13] For example at December 1969

	Bed sitters	1 b/r	2 b/r	3 b/r	4 b/r	Total
Family Housing Association	8	102	246	156	33	545
East London FHA	—	23	—	—	—	23
Notting Hill Housing Trust	72	173	105	50	25	425
Quadrant	23	40	189	85	8	345

[14] For a Director, General Manager, Housing Manager, Office Manager, Financial Executive, Development Manager, Surveyor, and Secretary.

the total cost of their administration was £40 000. Housing associations are thus compelled to acquire as many houses as possible in order to justify and fully utilize their administrative staff. The desire to acquire has in some cases been encouraged by the prospect of the development grant of £80 per property given by the GLC to cover administrative costs.

In Sutton the problems of expansion were much less evident and the need to employ professional housing management staff much less pressing. The CHA was run by volunteers and it was only in 1971 that the SHS found it necessary to employ a professional manager for the first time.

In Inner London more than Outer, the need to expand in order to be financially viable has also led to competition between housing associations for available property, yet some Inner London boroughs have an inadequate supply of property suitable for conversion.[15] Since few housing associations can be assured of an adequate regular supply of houses for conversion, their own building costs often tend to be higher since they cannot guarantee regular work. And because they are having to compete with other people for a steadily declining supply of houses, especially in 1970–71 when building society finance was plentiful, the associations are faced with the problem of not being able to achieve their targets or handle their waiting lists. Thus in November 1970 the FHA closed its list as there were already 800 families on it.[16] The LHT had had to take similar action in 1968.

In contrast with Lambeth, the Sutton associations do not seem to have been overwhelmed by the demand for accommodation and did not have to close their waiting lists. However, the SHS, which only built new dwellings, tended to have to compete with small local developers for available land. Both

[15] In May 1968, for example, the Director of the London Housing Trust wrote to the Director of Housing in Lambeth stressing that the Trust's progress in the borough had been pathetically slow. It had only actually purchased twelve units in its first year in Lambeth. This the Trust attributed to the limitations of the area to which they had been designated.
[16] When the Shelter Housing Aid Centre opened, seventy families in need of rehousing were coming to it every week. FHA, which had continued the link with the fatherless families section of SHAC, was only able to house about two per week.

were looking for 'infill' sites, and the fact that the associations could only pay the price for land determined by the District Valuer and were thereby open to being outbid, did restrict their activities.

This happened when the council offered a site to CHA. The Valuer would only allow them to pay £19 250 for it, despite the fact that the association offered £24 000. Meanwhile a private developer offered £27 000. On appeal the Valuer refused to alter his figure. This created a split on the council between the Health and Family Service Committee who still wanted to sell to the CHA and the Planning and Development Committee who wanted to sell to the highest bidder. The Ministry refused the council loan consent to borrow the £24 000 that CHA had offered as it exceeded the Valuer's figure. Consequently the site was lost. This would have been Castle-mead's first venture in new building. Also the Sutton associations found that estate agents were reluctant to deal with them as the property or land they acquired would never again be available for resale and consequently afford the agents the possibility of earning further fees.

What then was the result of the constraints affecting the goals of the two types of associations in the different areas?

Who did the Associations House?

Clearly the constraints on housing associations had a significant effect on their goals, particularly in Inner London. Firstly because of the working of the subsidy system the converted units provided by LHT, MHT, and FHA were mainly small ones.[17] Consequently the average household size was low. There were on average 1.16 and 1.06 children per household for LHT and MHT households respectively.[18] The average was 2.34 for

---

[17] See Appendix for details of samples.

[18] Despite the fact that LHT for instance had 128 households on its waiting list wanting three-bedroom flats and 22 households needing four- and five-bedroom flats. To some extent the Trust's waiting list reflected whom the Trust permitted to go on the waiting list, rather than the distribution of actual applicants, and it is likely that the Trust informed households of the improbability of their being housed and discouraged them from registering.

FHA because there were some larger families, probably due to FHA's connection with the Catholic Housing Aid Service and later the Shelter Housing Aid Centre. But 72 per cent of FHA's families had three children or less.

Secondly the financial constraints and rent levels meant that, despite their goal of helping families in housing need, neither LHT nor MHT housed many unskilled, unemployed or retired people (Table 3.1). FHA was somewhat more effective in most of these respects probably because it had specialized in housing unmarried mothers and fatherless families.

Table 3.1

Lambeth Housing Association Samples
Occupational Groups Housed by LHT, MHT, and FHA

Occupation	LHT	MHT	FHA
	%	%	%
Employers, managers, and professionals	4	0	2
Other white-collar workers	11	26	28
Service and semi-skilled manual workers	23	21	12
Foremen, skilled manual, and self-employed workers	26	19	14
Unskilled manual workers	5	9	14
Unemployed	4	3	17
Retired	9	3	0
No information	19	19	13
Total	100	100	100

(Totals may not add up to 100 exactly because of rounding.)

Sampling problems make it difficult to generalize about the income levels of families housed by the three associations but it is clear that they were not rehousing the poorest in the community. Thus between 1968 and 1971, whereas 60 per cent of the heads of households rehoused by the borough council were earning less than £20 per week, the corresponding proportion for LHT was 47 per cent. As the MHT did not have the advantage of the special arrangement between the borough and LHT whereby the borough gave rebates for all needy LHT tenants, not merely its own nominees, the incomes of MHT tenants during the same period were slightly higher than those in the LHT sample. FHA tenants had on average, lower incomes than either of the other two associations, probably because of their particular concern with one-parent families.

All this suggests that the associations did not house those in greatest need if this is defined in traditional local authority terms, i.e. unskilled and/or large families and the aged. Except possibly in the case of the FHA, in the past at least, this was not deliberate policy but a product of the constraints imposed on the associations.

However when the previous tenure of those housed by the associations was examined it became clear that they were complementing the local authority's role in providing for those who stood little chance of being in the council's housing programme for the reasons mentioned in Chapter One—the local authority's concentration on the areas which did not have high levels of multiple occupation, sharing, and insecure furnished accommodation, in order to make a 'housing gain'. Fifty per cent of the families housed by the LHT and 41 per cent of those housed by MHT had been living in furnished accommodation, and only 23 per cent (12 per cent) had been living in unfurnished privately-rented accommodation. None had been owner occupiers, and 14 per cent (13 per cent) had been illegal sub-tenants or living with their in-laws.[19] Sharing of amenities was high, 50 per cent of LHT tenants had shared a bath and 55 per cent had shared a w.c.[20]

Similarly, the largest single category of FHA tenants (52 per cent) had previously been living in furnished accommodation. Ten per cent had been the tenants of unfurnished premises, and 25 per cent had been living with in-laws, or as illegal subtenants. There were no owner occupiers. Their previous accommodation was likewise in most cases grossly inadequate for their needs. Fifty per cent of all the households shared a bath and 46 per cent shared a w.c.[21]

However, it could be argued that the FHA made a less valuable complementary contribution to meeting Lambeth's own needs because, as they received their loans from the GLC for the property they had acquired in Lambeth, FHA were not

---

[19] There was no information available about the previous tenure of 12 per cent (34 per cent) of the families.
[20] Unfortunately the information on sharing of amenities was not available for the MHT sample; there was no information in 75 per cent of the cases. There was no information in 48 per cent of the LHT cases.
[21] No information in 45 per cent of cases.

compelled to house applicants who were originally resident in Lambeth. In actual fact 37 per cent of the tenants had previously lived in Lambeth, and 13 per cent and 11 per cent in neighbouring Wandsworth and Southwark respectively. Eighty-six per cent of all the tenants had previously lived in Inner London.

Thus in Lambeth housing associations were broadly complementing the local authority's role of housing families who were generally manual workers, not technically the poorest of the community, in that they did not comprise the old or large families, yet families which were very apparently in housing need because their previous accommodation was insecure, i.e. furnished, and usually inadequate in facilities. These families would stand little chance of being helped by the local authority because they were neither registered on the waiting list nor living in typical clearance areas.

In Sutton the picture was markedly different. Of the forty households in the SHS sample, only four were two-person households, and in CHA all were one-person households. However, in contrast to the Lambeth associations, this was not the result of the constraints the associations faced but a result of their goals of catering for old people or the disabled. The remaining 12 per cent of tenants were senior white-collar or personal service workers, still in employment. All Castlemead's tenants were retired.[22] Because of the high number of retired people well over half (65 per cent) of Sutton Housing Society's tenants had an income of between £5–£9.99. Not one tenant had an income of over £25[23] but, as we have explained, these income levels did not affect the tenants' ability to pay the rent.

Finally the previous tenure categories and household amenities of the tenants showed far less of a contrast with what the local council was doing than in Lambeth. Tenures were more evenly distributed although living with in-laws was the largest category for Castlemead and the smallest for Sutton Housing Society. For Sutton Housing Society, furnished

---

[22] No information for 17 per cent of CHA tenants and 3 per cent of SHS tenants.
[23] No information for 3 per cent of CHA tenants and 5 per cent of SHS tenants.

tenancies were the largest category.[24] So far as amenities were concerned, 29 per cent of CHA (45 per cent of SHS) tenants shared a bath, and 29 per cent again of CHA (50 per cent of SHS) tenants shared a w.c.[25]

Thus the Sutton associations differed from the Lambeth associations in not housing those people who had a high degree of need but who were excluded from the council allocation process for a variety of reasons. For, as we saw in Chapter One, Sutton itself was beginning to specialize in housing old people and the disabled and it already housed a lot of people who had had to share amenities. Nevertheless they performed a useful role so far as the local authority was concerned for some at least of the elderly residents were being catered for without increasing the council-owned stock in the borough. They were not usually particularly poor but had often been living in accommodation unsuited to their needs, either because it was too large for them to maintain in widowhood, or too far from friends and relatives.

The Limitations of a Comprehensive Housing Policy

Despite the fact that Lambeth's associations ended up helping those who would not have been housed so quickly by the council, it is a wonder that they were successful in any way at all in view of the number of constraints they had to face.

Lambeth realized that, despite their stated aims of helping those in greatest need, the associations would be unlikely to be able to deal with many difficult cases such as families needing extensive social work support, large families, and those who could not pay regularly.[26] However, it was felt that the associations could, as we have seen, make a distinctive, though limited, contribution. The council therefore attempted to

---

[24] No information for 34 per cent of CHA tenants and 23 per cent of SHS tenants.

[25] No information for 58 per cent of CHA and 38 per cent of SHS tenants about baths; and no information for 54 per cent of CHA and 25 per cent of SHS tenants about w.cs.

[26] In its 'Community Plan' produced in 1971, Lambeth defined the object of housing associations as housing those in need of accommodation even though they may not necessarily be the poorest in the community.

minimize the constraints which might deflect the associations from performing this role.

A streamlined procedure for valuation and planning applications, a joint working party of all the council departments concerned, plus the negotiation for the largest associations of 'block loan sanctions', all helped to minimize delays in the acquisition of property and improve the competitive position of the housing associations in relation to other prospective purchasers.

The financial problems of the associations were eased in a number of ways. The council made a rate fund contribution of up to £100 per dwelling to bridge the gap between a cost rent and a 'fair rent' which is fixed for housing association units. In return the council requested the usual 50 per cent nomination rights to the lettings produced by housing associations. However, although the rents of the dwellings let to council nominees were rebated in accordance with the council's rebate scheme, as mentioned above, an additional experiment was undertaken in the largest association operating in the borough, the London Housing Trust: Lambeth agreed to rebate the rents of all London Housing Trust tenants in the borough (not just the rents of the borough's own nominees) where necessary. This enabled the LHT to house more of the really needy families.

However the borough did not control all the associations' activity in its area and therefore the total effect of the associations in the borough could not be harnessed to the particular conception of their strategic role that the Housing Department had. Nor had the initial actions of the Council in agreeing to support a large number of associations before closing the list helped the situation. In its evidence to the Cohen Committee on housing associations,[27] in 1968, the council expressed apprehension at the 'proliferation of housing associations with limited ability, limited experience, and limited objectives'. The local authority decided to rationalize the activities of housing associations by allocating an individual zone to each. However a sufficient number of areas free from planning proposals for the future thirty years could not be found for more than four of

---

[27] Department of the Environment, *Housing Associations* (London: H.M.S.O., 1971).

the largest housing associations and the remainder had to be allowed to purchase anywhere in the borough apart from the zoned areas. Even the zoned areas were insufficiently large to keep the designated housing associations fully occupied.

Many of the difficulties that Lambeth found in controlling housing associations in its area and ensuring that they fulfilled the role in the borough's attempt to mount a comprehensive policy, arose from the fact that many of the associations which created the problems were financed by the GLC. The GLC had a very different conception of a comprehensive housing policy and of the role of housing associations.

When the GLC was under Labour control from 1965–67 it supported housing associations only if they could not get borough council funds. The Conservatives on gaining office dropped this provision and greatly expanded their support for the associations from under £1m in 1967–68 to a projected £25m per annum in the three years from 1970 onwards.[28] In addition, apart from making a rate fund contribution to bridge the deficit between a cost rent and a 'fair rent', the GLC made a grant of £80 per dwelling to meet administrative costs. These decisions were a product of the Conservatives' preference for private, or at least 'non-public' housing[29] evident in their chapter on housing in the Greater London Development Plan. The increased allocation of funds bore no apparent relationship to the then level of demand from the associations or their capacity to absorb the available money. In fact the GLC Director of Housing made this clear when he told the GLDP Inquiry that he was allocated far more money than he had requested.[30]

Particular advantages to housing associations of negotiating

---

[28] GLC Minutes, 27 January, 1970. Significantly, although a great increase in the amount to be allocated to housing associations was made, the remaining housing expenditure by the GLC was to be kept stable at £60m per annum.

[29] In fact Horace Cutler, at one time chairman of the GLC Housing Committee, is on record as recommending that houses with controlled tenancies should be bought by local authorities and handed over to housing associations for rehabilitation. Afterwards the houses could be offered back to the landlord at a favourable purchase price.

[30] Transcript of the Greater London Development Plan Inquiry, 37th day, Friday, 18 December, 1970, p. 67.

with the GLC included not only the availability of funds and the favourable financial conditions but also the fact that an agreement with the GLC standardized the housing associations' conditions of operation throughout the whole of London. If housing associations negotiated with individual borough councils, they had to negotiate a separate agreement with each borough in whose area they wished to operate with its loans. However, the GLC was anxious to disburse the money allocated to the voluntary housing movement even if this conflicted with what the borough councils wanted. Theoretically, the GLC wanted to encourage different housing associations to concentrate on specific geographical areas but the bigger associations did not want to be limited in this fashion. Some such as the Notting Hill Housing Trust and Paddington Churches Housing Trust came to an agreement between themselves over respective territories, but larger associations such as Quadrant and Family Housing Association operated anywhere possible because of their need to continue purchasing in order to offset administrative costs. Since housing associations receiving GLC loans only had to ensure that tenants were Londoners, rather than residents of the borough in which the association's dwellings were situated, this could cause further conflict with the borough council, especially in a borough like Lambeth which had a conscious policy of trying to encourage households to leave the borough where possible. The entry into the borough of new families housed in properties acquired by GLC supported housing associations (as in the case of our FHA sample) exacerbated the borough's problems, although the associations were admittedly helping to improve the physical fabric of the housing stock in the borough. Lambeth insisted that housing associations to which it lent money must not borrow from the GLC as well, but it could not prevent other associations from purchasing in the borough with GLC loans.[31] Attempts by the Town Clerk in September 1969, and by the Director of Housing in July 1970 to persuade the GLC not to finance additional housing associations operating in the borough proved fruitless.

---

[31] FHA, for example, had bought about 130 units in Lambeth with GLC money by 1970, including some in the Josephine Avenue area, zoned to the London Housing Trust, much to the latter's chagrin.

In addition, as Lambeth insisted in its conditions for assistance that housing associations must not pay more for a property than the council valuation, it could prevent the price of houses rising owing to the competition between housing associations. However it is claimed by other housing associations that the GLC valuer has been valuing property at £200–£300 more than the borough valuer and has thereby been encouraging the inflationary spiral in house prices.

Unlike Lambeth, the GLC's attitude towards the role of housing associations did not fit in with a broader planning policy of catering for different types of households. The GLC's interest in housing associations arose from its concern to increase the part played by private enterprise and non-council institutions in the housing market. It was related to the other aspects of GLC housing policy such as the increase of mortgage funds for owner occupation and the reduction of the council house building programme. The GLC was not concerned with analysing what types of households would increasingly lose out as a result of such an emphasis in housing policy. Thus just as the allocation of the funds to housing associations was on a rather random first come, first served basis, with little inquiry as to how housing associations proposed to select tenants, or whom they considered themselves to be catering for, so the GLC's own nominations to housing association vacancies were rather random. In the final analysis if it proved too expensive the GLC opted out of its privilege to nominate.[32]

In the period 1969–71 Sutton made loans to ten housing associations mainly catering for old people. It also made a rate fund contribution and reserved nomination rights to 25 per cent of the dwellings in the old people's schemes and 50 per cent in the few general needs schemes. As we have seen, Sutton encouraged associations to specialize in the needs of old people. In this respect, Sutton had continued the traditional role per-

---

[32] As happened, for example, in the case of the Barnsbury Housing Association in Islington. Here the GLC had 75 per cent nomination rights, but it decided eventually not to take advantage of these because the high rents would have necessitated too high a rebate for GLC nominees. Rents ranged from £450 a year exclusive of rates for a one-bedroomed unit to £600 for three bedrooms. GLC Minutes, 23 June, 1970, Questions 14 and 15.

formed by housing associations prior to the real growth of the voluntary housing movement. If anything Sutton's policy reflected the GLC's attitude in that it reduced the necessity to rely on the public sector to meet this particular need.

Despite the fact that Sutton undoubtedly recognized a strategic role for the associations there is evidence that they had not pursued the implications of this to the same extent that Lambeth did. They did not streamline the process of application by housing associations. Initial applications came to the Deputy Town Clerk who passed them onto the Assistant Borough Architect, who acted as the liaison officer between departments for housing associations. The delay which resulted from this procedure meant that associations frequently lost sites or properties to speculative developers of prospective owner occupiers. Fortunately in Sutton there were comparatively few, if any, GLC-backed associations operating on a large scale.

To summarize, in Lambeth, Sutton, and the GLC, the associations performed a definite and distinctive role in the housing policies of the authorities. The constraints facing the associations—of competing for land and housing with limited finance—were as significant as any of their ideologies in determining which people would benefit from the associations' activities. In Lambeth, additional constraints were imposed by the operations of GLC-backed associations. Lambeth, with some success, attempted to minimize the constraints which might have prevented the associations fulfilling their role in a comprehensive policy. Sutton was less effective in this respect, but the constraints facing Sutton's associations were not so overwhelming.

The different kinds of 'comprehensive' housing policy emerge quite clearly from the operations of the housing associations. As in Chapter One the problems of Lambeth are most significant and the limitations of local authorities working in confined geographical areas most evident. We can see again the conflicts which arise from different conceptions of what a 'comprehensive' housing policy involves. If housing associations are to play a 'comprehensive' role then we must be sure whose definition of 'comprehensive' we are talking about.

Chapter Four

Building Societies

Background

Building societies, both individually and collectively, have emerged as organizations of increasing importance in the housing market in recent years. According to the Chief Registrar of Friendly Societies [1], the movement grew by £6400m, or 222 per cent between 1960 and 1969, and in 1969 the assets of the two largest societies (the Abbey National and the Halifax) alone exceeded the assets of the whole movement in 1959. Building societies in general are now second only to the banks as major financial institutions and they loan two-thirds of the money used to finance house purchase.[1] At the same time building societies have increased their individual power by a series of mergers which have reduced the number of societies by 30 per cent in ten years, from 732 to 503 [1]. However it is less clear who has benefited from all this growth. Who, in other words, have building societies been trying to serve and to what extent do they follow purely economic market forces or to what extent do they try to do something more?

We have seen that local authorities, to a greater or lesser extent, try to intervene in, or compensate for the operations of market forces by building houses or providing mortgages not necessarily with a view to making a profit. Similarly the study of housing associations shows that they try to do this too. Building societies themselves are not allowed to make profits as such but, as with some housing associations and local authorities,

---

[1] 'Recent Development in Housing Statistics', *Economic Trends*, November 1968, p. 15. The remaining third included insurance companies (8 per cent), inheritance or gift (10 per cent), local authorities (6 per cent), cash or other loan (10 per cent).

it is equally difficult to discover at first glance whether they are 'socially-oriented' organizations or not. When building societies increase interest rates in line with rising interest rates in other savings institutions, for instance, they could well be acting to protect their investors, or they could be doing so reluctantly in order to ensure that future borrowers have sufficient funds, or they could equally be trying to ensure their own survival—by preventing panic withdrawals. In other words, a challenge from other institutions could be a constraint on the operations of building societies if the aim of the societies is to provide cheap home loans. On the other hand, such a challenge need not be a constraint if the societies are solely concerned with the interests of investors or if they are intent on personal survival to the exclusion of all else. In fact what we have to say will show that, after looking at local authorities and housing associations, the study of building societies brings us one step closer to a study of the operations of pure market forces in the organization of housing.

Their Aims and Organization

In a recent study an attempt was made to distinguish between three different sorts of ideological view-points that businessmen might hold [2]. They were: (1) the *laissez-faire* attitude (LF)—here taken to mean that all that matters is to maximize profits, (2) the long-term company interest attitude (LTCI)—which claims that in the end the best profit could be maintained by the firm behaving in a socially responsible way, and (3) the social responsibility attitude (SR)—which saw the main purpose of the firm as giving service to society. In practice most business-men rejected (1) and could not distinguish between (2) and (3), rejecting the more instrumental attitudes in the LTCI ideology and the more idealistic ones in the SR ideology. It is this mixture of attitudes that building society executives hold, the connection between their social claims and the claims of business being a very close one. One executive told us for instance that their objective was 'the promotion of thrift and home ownership'. Another society claimed to be aiming at a wider social composition among its mortgagors than other societies. Yet another told us that they wanted to lend more on older property than was normal and another that they were the first to offer easy lending terms to newly marrieds. However, the General Manager of the Bristol and West Building Society has been quoted as saying that societies are 'run as commercial enterprises and not as extensions of the welfare state' [3].

Building societies are peculiar institutions if viewed as commercial enterprises. They borrow short to lend long, an exact reversal of the normal pattern of financial institutions and one which requires that they place a great stress on retaining the confidence of investors. Therefore risk taking, which is usually a central part of successful private enterprise, is wholly alien to the money-lending activities of the movement. According to the Chief Registrar of Friendly Societies Annual Report for 1969 [1], for example, under 1 per cent of the total balances of the societies due on mortgages were more than twelve months in arrears in that year. In other words, the need to attract what could turn out to be only short-term deposits, means that strict safeguards must be placed on lending policies. Any attempt to lend on older property or to different groups of people does not mean that the societies concerned are significantly different from others, only that they are trying to 'carve out' a new slice of the market for themselves, either because they are relatively small or new societies, or because they have a possible surplus of funds and a strong enough base from which to branch out. Smaller societies and those lending on older property will generally charge more to borrowers so that they can in turn pay more to depositors. The overriding consideration of the societies becomes, therefore, trying to retain investors' confidence by paying them an adequate, secure, competitive return on the money they lend for house purchase.

These aims and considerations are reflected in the internally self-perpetuating recruitment system and the minimal delegation of power in the societies' operations. The main source of recruitment to the societies is still teenage grammar school leavers and most promotions are from within the organizations.[2] In the building society world the General Manager who began

---

[2] An article in the July 1971 Building Societies Institute Quarterly draws attention to the declining proportion of male school-leavers who are going into clerical jobs and their replacement by women. 'Many of the traditional sources of recruitment of building society staff, such as grammar schools, are now drying up as more and more students go on to

as a clerk in the same company forty years earlier is still the rule rather than the exception. Even transfers between societies are frowned upon—we were told this was 'poaching'—unless the move is to a senior post in a smaller society. Few people are brought in from outside even to the top echelons of management. The Building Societies Institute does provide an increasing number of professional training courses but they are mainly attended by middle and upper management. Many of the larger building societies still train their junior staff themselves and we were told that the purpose of this was to indoctrinate them with the particular outlook and operating procedures of their company. Most applicants for a loan are likely to have their main contact with a society via the branch manager and most societies recruit their managers from the more junior staff. Very rarely, if ever, are managers brought in from outside the organization. Our interviews with branch managers showed that they had a limited amount of discretion but were prepared to bend the rules or interpret them in different ways according to the particular needs of the areas they serve. For example, in areas where there is very little new housing a branch manager is likely to be more willing to lend on older property than in an area where there is a lot of new housing. However the basic outlook of the managers and other staff is a conservative one and appears to be inculcated at an early stage in their professional training. The values and attitudes to matters such as risk taking, security, and status which we outline in this chapter are rarely questioned and, we suspect, very difficult to alter.

An additional factor is that managers are assessed by the contribution they can make to investment. The powers and duties of the branch managers vary from society to society but one common element is this primary responsibility for attracting investment. Indeed in one society we interviewed this was their sole duty, plus interviewing—though not approving—candidates for loans. It is more usual for the manager to have power

colleges and universities. As the decade progresses building societies may find themselves appointing an increasing number of graduates to their staff. An increasing number of women will also probably be found in managerial positions.' D. Lee. 'The Main Problems Facing Building Societies in the 1970s', *BSI Quarterly*, Vol. 25, No. 99, p. 146.

to approve up to a limit of, say, £10 000 but even in societies where this happens the value of the manager is often measured by the investment he attracts. Thus in one very large society the amount of funds available to a manager to lend depends, in part, on the amount of investment he attracts. The key qualities that a manager is expected to have are an ability to forge useful links with the business and professional community. These people introduce many new investors and in turn are often (if they are estate agents for example) rewarded for their efforts by an informal quota from the society.

This accountability of branch managers for investment is accompanied by the fact that people at the top of the societies— at board level—have a considerable part to play in the lending operations of the societies. The boards of directors tend to meet either in full or in sub-committee (in the larger societies) weekly or fortnightly. They have the power to decide policy and are quite closely concerned with the day-to-day affairs of even the largest societies. For example, in two of the larger societies (which we interviewed) all loans over £25 000 had to be approved by the Board and in one of them, loans in the range of £15 000 to £25 000 had to be approved by a director. In one of the middle range societies we interviewed (assets of about £50m) the power to approve *all* mortgages was vested in the three top managers.

The aim of the societies to ensure stability as investment media is thus clearly enhanced by their organizational structure which involves internal 'indoctrination' and training and minimal delegation of decision making. We are left with the question of whether there were any constraints at all on what building societies could do.

The Constraints Facing the Societies

The main constraints relate to the system of controls which govern the operations of building societies and which make any attempt to compete with one another by 'carving out' new markets a limited one.

The Building Societies Act of 1962 is the major statute governing the operations of the movement, consolidating and extending nine previous Acts. However the modern framework of legislation was created by its predecessor, the 1960 Act. The

effect of these Acts has been to tighten the control over the
societies by the Chief Registrar of Friendly Societies. Significantly the main reasons why this was thought to be necessary
were almost entirely the results of concern with ensuring that
societies were safe investment media rather than developments
in the role of the agencies as lenders of money. As Cleary says,
'existing legislation was proving itself incapable of curbing the
activities of certain societies. These societies presented themselves to potential investors as normal building societies, but
used the money invested with them to finance property trans-
actions far removed from the bulk of normal building society
lending' [4]. In fact it was the collapse of the State Building
Society through the failure of a takeover bid for a property
company that finally provoked action.

The main powers given to the Registrar by this Act are
(in his words) 'to control the building societies' activities in the
interests of persons who are or may become investors or
depositors in the society'.[3] The Act also tried to extend the
rights of members to play an active part in the societies'
operations by a number of means but, as Cleary states, 'building
society boards are for all practical purposes self perpetuating
groups' and he adds, more controversially in our view, 'because
it is so difficult for the shareholders to exercise control, the
Registrar has to assume the role of shareholders' representative' [5]. In fact our interviews with several societies and with
the Registrar himself showed that the Act's investor-oriented,
safety first ethic is shared to a great extent by the staff of
societies. The Chief Registrar only really exercises his power
against a very few small dishonest or incompetently run
societies and even then apparently 90 per cent of his work is
done on an informal basis—'giving the directors a pep talk'.
The Registrar also serves as an authority on whether innovations
which are suggested by societies (invariably on the investment
side) are legal. Thus he was consulted recently before societies

---

[3] The powers enable the Registrar to stop a society accepting investments, to stop or control advertising, to specify the way in which surplus
funds may be invested, to make regulations regarding the form and
content of the balance sheet, to require an annual return with such
information as the Registrar may request, to approve amalgamations,
and to carry out effective investigations of societies' affairs.

introduced property bond and linked life investment schemes.[4]

The control which the Chief Registrar has over the societies is heavily reinforced, and is complementary to, the control that the Building Societies Association (BSA) has over them. The BSA is the trade association of the movement and it usually represents the building society movement in negotiations with the government. The vast majority of the building societies, and all the larger societies, belong to it. It is quite a disciplined organization and requirements for membership are even more stringent than those laid down by the Chief Registrar.

The BSA exercises its authority by checking the accounts of building societies every year and it can throw out members who have committed misdemeanours. The Association has very close informal links with the Registrar and if they notice societies getting into trouble they will alert the Registrar to this fact if they deem it necessary, and he in turn may use them to bring pressure to bear on the societies who are carrying out activities he is doubtful about. The BSA is active in disseminating information and technical advice but it does not recommend any new departures from the existing policy.

However, so far as the lending side of operations are concerned, we were told by the BSA that the societies regard this very much as their own prerogative and would not welcome direct interference from the Association. Most of the recent innovations on the investment side have similarly come from individual societies rather than from the BSA. What the BSA does is insist that in order to qualify for membership, societies fulfil the requirements of 'trustee' status.[5] It is concerned that

---

[4] These schemes use life assurance and property development as inducement to get investors to, at the same time, put some of their money in the societies. They evade the clauses in the 1962 Building Societies Act barring the societies from themselves doing this sort of business by working the scheme in association with other companies who, notionally, take the money and then invest it in the societies.

[5] Under the Housing (Financial Provisions) Act 1958 central government and local authorities were prepared to guarantee amounts lent by societies on older houses in excess of the amounts that they would normally have lent. The societies involved had to qualify for 'trustee status' so far as investment in those societies was concerned.

The Registrar was given the power to decide who should qualify. The conditions included assets of at least £5m and liquid assets of not less

the society should have a higher liquidity ratio (i.e. the ratio of cash and investments to total assets) than the Registrar insists on. In 1970 the average liquidity ratio of the societies was running at about 18 per cent compared with the liquidity ratio of 7½ per cent required by the Registrar. Thus the BSA reinforces the legislative controls by ensuring that most of the societies comply with the requirements of good business without the necessity for the external intervention of the Registrar.

It is clear that the Registrar feels that the 'social' role of the societies and their economic significance are not his concern. If anyone has responsibility for these it is the Department of the Environment and the Treasury respectively. The lack of control of these two Ministries is however more evident than its presence. Two factors which often concern politicians are the level of interest rates charged to borrowers and the type of property for which loans are granted. The last Labour government's concern with the former point led to a reference of building societies' charges to the Prices and Incomes Board [6]. The societies were able to argue that the level of interest they charged was a reasonable one but eventually they did agree to some reduction of the liquidity ratio.[6] However the Registrar

---

than 7½ per cent of total assets. Free reserves plus funds set aside to meet capital losses on investments had to be at least 2½ per cent of total assets.

The 1958 scheme ended in 1961 but the recognition of trustee status is still awarded by the Registrar and is a mark of the respectability of a society. The officially defined qualifications for trustee status have, in fact, always been well below those required by the Building Societies Association for membership. For further details see, Cleary, op. cit., p. 256.

[6] The PIB report referred to above concluded that 'the minimum reserve and liquidity ratios laid down by the BSA as a qualification for membership and broadly adopted by the Government as a qualification for trustee status, are not based on a statistical assessment of risk. If these requirements are tested against the actual course of events over recent years there is a prima-facie case for suggesting that the minima are higher than they need to be. Moreover, the reserve and liquidity ratios actually maintained by societies are well in excess of these minima.' (Chapter 9, Summary and Conclusions, p. 31.)

Rather than make detailed recommendations the PIB suggested that the BSA set up its own enquiry to see how the requirements should be altered. This the BSA did and they subsequently altered their reserve ratio requirement so that it now is a declining percentage of total assets

told us that he would only investigate a society charging a higher interest rate if it was being done because the money was being lent on riskier property, e.g. older or tenanted houses which were poor security for investors. If people are prepared to pay 10 per cent interest rate on a house which the Abbey National, for example, would lend on at 8½ per cent this does not concern the Chief Registrar—he certainly has no duty to the public to advise them on these matters.

This emphasis on accountability to investors and limited concern for the borrowers has been clearly indicated to us by the societies' staff. When asked about how the social responsibility part of this ethic is operationalized the commonest answers seem to be firstly, those that relate to the refusal to charge 'what the market will bear' in interest rates and secondly, the undoubted trouble that many societies take to ease the problems of those who fall into arrears with their repayments. We do not think that it is cynical to suggest that these policies, which are socially valuable, are pursued because it is in the long term company interest to do so. It seems highly improbable that successive governments would continue to grant the movement privileges such as reduced tax liability and a special legal position if they had tried to maximize interest rates. It is also clear that no societies relish the adverse publicity that court cases for possession and eviction of mortgagors in arrears bring, with the possibility of scaring away investors. We were struck by the uniformity of expression of this 'sort of social consciousness' (as the Registrar called it) in the various societies we investigated.

In effect then the constraints as such are not very great, perhaps the most significant one being the government's attempt to keep mortgages as cheap as possible. The ideology behind the activities of the Chief Registrar and the Building Societies Association is supported with a few reservations by societies.

---

as the overall size of the society involved increases. The PIB suggestion that liquidity ratios could be reduced has been ignored. The average liquidity ratio of UK building societies has risen from 15·4 in 1960 to 18·2 in the third quarter of 1971. The societies argue that they are building up funds to deal with future demand.

Who Got the Building Society Mortgages?

Because of the concern with the interests of investors, the essential elements in the allocation of mortgages are considerations of the security of property and status of applicant.

The simplest way of illustrating what security means is to say that the ideally secure property is one which is new or recently built, is a house rather than a flat or maisonnette, and is not more than two storeys high. Status, however, is an ill-defined term but we were assured that it is not a value-laden concept. It is some measure of a person's capacity to pay which also, in our experience, is related to their age and likely stability of future earnings. The ideal type for the societies would be a young professional with a secure job and guaranteed annual increments. Blue-collar workers are at a disadvantage, not only for the obvious reasons that their earnings may be low (as Barbolet showed they may be comparable to those of some white-collar workers) [7] but because the future level and stability of their earnings is, or is thought to be, in doubt. It is not clear how far purely subjective factors affect decisions but one manager said that he was impressed by people who had 'worked things out', which suggests that the prospective buyer who did not have this ability might be at a disadvantage. It seems to us that managers build up an image in their minds of what qualifies an applicant, some part of which may be purely objective, e.g. income level, and some part of which seems purely subjective, e.g. societies do not like 100 per cent mortgages because they suspect that people without savings may be incapable of paying regularly. The fact that these people have probably been regularly paying high rents seems to be ignored. Once again the problem of the marginal buyer in Inner London, moving between jobs with little spare capacity for savings, paying high rents and transport costs is obvious. Additional limitations are caused by the refusal of most societies to grant mortgages which will run past retirement.[7] One of the societies we investigated does offer a thirty-five year

---

[7] This should be compared with other countries, e.g. Australia, where the value of the house not the age of the borrower is paramount and such a practice is common.

term on new houses but borrowers over thirty are unlikely to qualify. This attitude should be contrasted with that of many local authorities who lend on the security of the property rather than the person, realizing that even if the mortgagor does die before the term is completed the value of the house will have effectively guaranteed their loan.

In addition the option mortgage scheme which is supposed to help poorer buyers paying less than the standard rate of income tax is rarely used in London. We have been told that this is because the income required to buy property which is mortgageable usually exceeds the low level at which standard rate income tax begins to be paid. Hence the mortgagor cannot gain by choosing the option scheme because his income is basically inadequate in the first place.

Until recently the available funds have been oversubscribed. In this situation a further allocation procedure operates to the disadvantage of the marginally qualified. Many societies give high priority to existing clients who are selling their houses in order to buy another. It is often essential—for those who do not have large deposits—to save with the societies for some time before getting a loan, especially when there is a very heavy demand for funds. Also, as we have shown, quotas may be given to estate agents, brokers, and others so that the chance of getting a loan may depend on the professionals involved in the transaction. An ability to comprehend and operate within this quite complex allocation system is very important.

When we look at the data we collected we can see the building societies' concern with security and status reflected in who gets mortgages. Table 4.1 summarizes the main characteristics of the people to whom all the building societies operating in London lent money. The Department of the Environment data does not contain details of the occupations of borrowers.[8] But one of the large societies we looked at had data available which did show the socio-economic groups of its mortgagors.

As we would expect, the average income (for 1970) is quite high and the purchase price of housing was correspondingly high too. If we combine some details of Table 4.1 with the

---

[8] See the Appendix for details of sampling.

Table 4.1

Building Society Samples
DoE 5 per cent sample survey 1970. All societies lending
money in Greater London

	Property in	
	Inner London* (Group A boroughs)	Outer London* (Group B boroughs)
Number of mortgages in sample	325	1539
Average purchase price of property	£7593	£6731
Average term of loan	20 years	22 yrs 3 mths
Average income of borrowers	£2632	£2362
Median income of borrowers	£2242	£2122
Average age of borrowers	36	34
Previous tenure of borrowers		
(a) Owner occupiers	24%	32%
(b) Private renters	38%	27%
(c) Local authority renters	3%	3%
(d) Others (i.e. new households)	15%	20%
(e) No information	18%	15%

* See the Introduction for the division of Inner and Outer London as Group A and B boroughs.

information on occupations mentioned above, it is apparent that borrowers in London are older, professionally employed persons or young, high-earning couples. Managers and professional workers accounted for 38 per cent of the loans given by the larger society which kept the occupational data of its borrowers, and although 20 per cent of its mortgagors were service workers, and 30 per cent manual workers, the income distributions of these groups show that these people were definitely among the high-earning groups in these occupations. The income distribution of the service workers corresponded to the distribution of income among all borrowers, suggesting that it is only the higher paid service workers who are getting loans. The vast majority of manual workers were foremen, supervisors or skilled workers.

Table 4.1 also shows that many London buyers already had a house and were presumably able to put down a substantial deposit. In fact the borrowers who were already owner occupiers bought substantially more expensive houses than those in other tenure groups. Very few buyers, no matter what their previous tenure, obtained the really long mortgages that marginal purchasers are likely to require. Less than 1 per cent of all loans were for more than twenty-five years in Inner London, and less than 5 per cent in Outer London.

However, one of the most important features which emerges from Table 4.1 is that practically five times as many mortgages were given in Outer as compared to Inner London. Older and cheaper property does exist in Inner London (and in Outer London too), as we saw when we discussed the local authority schemes, but societies are reluctant to lend on it especially when, as will often be the case, applicants have low incomes, no deposits, and want high percentage loans.

The option mortgage scheme is intended to help buyers with low incomes to enter the owner occupation sector if the price of the house they wish to buy is below a certain ceiling. The guarantee part of the scheme allows for up to 20 per cent of the valuation to be added to what the building society will offer and it is possible to get a total mortgage of up to 100 per cent of valuation—the excess percentage granted above the amount the societies would normally lend being backed by a government guarantee. However only about 5 per cent of borrowers in the DoE sample had option mortgages and none of these were for 100 per cent with guarantee. The complete absence of 100 per cent mortgages suggests that the societies' dislike for people with no deposits prevails even when the risk involved no longer falls on the society but is met by central government. It also reflects the low initial percentage granted by building societies, for in order for people to receive 100 per cent mortgages under the guaranteed scheme building societies have to advance initially 80 per cent. In fact less than 4 per cent of the mortgages granted were over 95 per cent of valuation and the average advance was 70 per cent of the valuation.

The four societies we looked at in detail did not deviate significantly from the general pattern of lending by all societies in London, although there are some interesting differences.

All our societies lent in both Inner and Outer London. However one society only had one mortgage in Inner London and six in Outer London. This lack of London lending by the very society that initially seemed to be the closest we could find to a locally based company,[9] bears out that society's expressed

---

9 See Appendix.

dislike for the older property which must form the main bulk of any business in London.

Another of our societies, according to the DoE data, certainly appeared to specialize in the sort of older property available in Inner London. It only had assets of £50m yet had more loans in the Inner London sample than either of the other two societies with assets ten and thirteen times as great. One of these two societies prided itself on its attempts to encourage a wide spectrum of the community to become owner occupiers and was one of the first societies to introduce thirty-five year mortgages. Its executives told us that, although they had no evidence, they felt that they probably had a wider social composition among their mortgagors than many other societies. However the data challenged this claim showing that the average and median incomes of this society's borrowers in Inner London are higher than the figures for the main sample and considerably higher in both Inner and Outer London than those for the other large society which did not make any special claims and did, if anything, make it clear that they were not in the market for those on lower wages and salaries, preferring to leave such people and the houses they bought to the local authorities. However this society seemed to have a somewhat more liberal earnings rule than the other societies and this probably explains the differences in their income figures.

In conclusion, the data does bear out some of the claims made by the societies in our interviews with them although not all that the societies claimed appears proven. More importantly it shows that, despite general similarities in the lending patterns, these patterns do vary to some extent. Consequently the ability to choose the right society to approach for a loan may well be crucial to the buyer who is marginal in terms of security or status.

The Limitations of a Comprehensive Housing Policy

Both Sutton and the GLC are strongly committed to furthering owner occupation and both have their own mortgage schemes. However neither of these authorities have thought it necessary to attempt to influence the operations of building societies in their respective areas whereas Lambeth has made such an attempt. Apart from the evident lack of Lambeth's broad interpretation of its housing responsibilities on the part of the other two authorities it might also be added that Sutton is an attractive area for the societies to lend in already, so no particular interference from the local authority is required.

As we have seen Lambeth and the rest of Inner London does not get the benefit of much building society finance—one executive told us that although many people in Lambeth invested in his society, this money was loaned on houses elsewhere. So the Director of Housing invited executives from five societies (including our two smaller societies) together with the Secretary-General of the BSA to meet him. He urged the societies to start savings schemes for young couples which would guarantee them a mortgage (a similar scheme to that proposed by Julian Amery to the BSA at a later date). He also urged them to lend on the cost of improving older housing and there was discussion about the possibility of the council guaranteeing loans in excess of those that a society would normally give to an applicant of a given status and on property of a given security. In effect this would be like the 1958 Housing (Financial Provisions) Act scheme except that none of the additional liability would be borne by the society. However the main purpose of the meeting was to encourage societies to lend more in Lambeth which, inevitably, means lending more on older properties. The risk on this would be minimal as the council intended to declare and implement a very large programme of General Improvement Areas, as we saw in Chapter One. Apart from safeguarding the properties in such areas from clearance or redevelopment, the environmental improvements carried out by the council after the declaration of these areas should ensure a rapid appreciation in the value of the properties within them. Lambeth was prepared to suggest that people who wanted to buy in the borough should invest in societies that were financing house purchase in these areas. The bargain proposed was that the societies would get investment in exchange for a loan quota which would be available for the Housing Advice Centre to use.[10]

---

[10] The Shelter Housing Aid Centre has a somewhat similar arrangement with several societies—the difference is that the money is mainly used for new housing in Outer London or beyond.

To date little has come from this initiative and, in the light of our interviews with societies and their association, we doubt whether it will ever bear much fruit. One of the societies thought that the 1969 Housing Act and the emphasis on improvement was wrong-headed and that the answer to the housing problem lay in the production of new houses. One of our societies said that they would never take the initial risk of investing in a GIA. Their subsequent reference to Islington as an 'improving area' made us feel that they would not in fact be very willing to lend in an older area until 'gentrification' had gone so far that prices were way beyond the means of most would-be buyers. Anyway this society, in common with the other societies we interviewed, would only consider investment in GIA's if they had money to spare, i.e. if their traditional market was saturated. Even then they would be far more likely to save the money in the expectation of renewed demand at some later point from this market. One only needs to be mildly cynical to see this as something that any business might do if demand fell in its traditional market.

Despite the willingness of one of our smaller societies to co-operate with Lambeth in a guarantee scheme the main problem facing Lambeth in negotiating with the societies is that their selection process for loans is dominated by the fact that there is generally no shortage of 'normal' applicants. It is clear from our interviews that this is in itself a major obstacle to any liberalization of the rules which govern who gets the money. If the traditional tried and tested market provides more than enough business there can be no commercial rationale for diverting any of the resources from this market. While it is true that different societies have marginally different rules the similarities appear to be greater than the differences. Despite the societies' claim that they never had enough money to satisfy all their customers, by 1972 they certainly had more available than at any previous time, and we had some indication of a certain amount of slackening in the income criteria that they used to calculate the maximum allowable loan. But in a market in which prices are increasing rapidly these marginal adjustments would be unlikely to alter to any great extent the type of person eligible for a loan.

Thus our analysis of the operations of the societies suggests that they are, so far as their lending operations are concerned, quite conservative and unlikely to be in the forefront of any move to extend their services to marginal buyers or older properties to the extent required for any significant increase in lending in areas like Lambeth to be meaningful. Furthermore this attitude is reinforced by successive governments in legislation and in the way in which the societies' business is regulated by the Chief Registrar of Friendly Societies. Although the ideological outlook of societies is very conservative, the constraining influence of the Chief Registrar threatens any serious attempt by a society to 'carve out' a significantly new market should the incentives from a borough like Lambeth be adequate in terms of promised investment. Generally it is the ideology of building societies which constrains marginal buyers but the Chief Registrar acts as a further constraint both on building societies and marginal buyers.

Governments try to encourage building societies to keep mortgage rates down because both political parties are wedded to the idea of home ownership. But governments are noticeably inconsistent when dealing with the societies. The situation may arise where a Chancellor of the Exchequer wants to encourage saving in order to control inflation. Building societies follow the general trends of rising interest rates in competition with other savings institutions. Central government then tries to persuade the Building Societies Association not to recommend to its members the higher lending rate which the societies consider they need to enable them to pay the higher rate to depositors. Any attempts by the government or any other central body, such as the Prices and Incomes Board, to get societies to take alternative measures such as reducing their liquidity ratios have been extremely half-hearted, probably in recognition of the fact that building societies act primarily as savings institutions in pursuit of the goals of security, reliability, and stability.

In order for building societies to take part in a comprehensive strategy either at central government or local government level they would have to be changed from investor-oriented, non-risk taking quasi-commercial enterprises. For these reasons Lambeth's attempt to enlist the co-operation of the societies seems bound to be of marginal importance. Areas such as Sutton will continue to provide a much more attractive market for the societies.

References

1. *Report of the Chief Registrar of Friendly Societies for 1969*, Part 2, 'Building Societies' (London: H.M.S.O., 1970).

2. NICHOLS, T. *Ownership, Control, and Ideology* (London: Allen and Unwin, 1969).

3. BREACH, A. 'The political scene', *Investors Chronicle and Stock Exchange Gazette*, 15 May, 1970.

4. CLEARY, E. J. *The Building Societies Movement* (London: Elek, 1965), p. 260.

5. Ibid., p. 266.

6. National Board for Prices and Incomes. *Rate of Interest on Building Society Mortgages*. Report No. 22, Cmnd 3136 (London: H.M.S.O., 1966).

7. BARBOLET, R. H. *Housing Classes and the Socio-ecological System*. University Working Paper No. 4 (London: Centre for Environmental Studies, 1969).

Chapter Five

Private Landlords and Estate Agents

Background

Despite the commonly expressed hope that the housing association movement would be a 'third arm' supplanting the
privately-rented sector, we saw in Chapter Three how a whole
series of constraints restricted the output of the associations and
prevented them from achieving the size that would be required
if they were to assume this role.

Therefore the main alternative to publicly rented or owner-
occupied housing remains private renting. However the contribution of private landlords has diminished drastically since
the turn of the century.[1] Central and local government have

---

[1] The reasons for the decline are well documented. Firstly, the growth of
building societies and local authorities since the early years of this century
has provided a serious challenge to the private landlord as the main
provider of accommodation. In addition, the person buying property for
his own occupation receives tax relief on the investment he pays on his
mortgage and at the current rate of inflation pays very little in real terms
for the property. If he sells the property he can also make a tax-free
capital gain. An increasing proportion of the population have benefited
from the advantage of tax relief as the standard rate of income tax is now
paid by most households at some point in their lives. Finally, there has
been a lack of any steady flow of capital for private landlords, and landlords have not been able to obtain tax relief on funds used to amortize
loans, or on money set aside to cover depreciation. This places the
owner of rented property at a disadvantage compared to people with
other kinds of investment.

For further discussion, see Appendix V of the Milner Holland Report,
and also Greve, J. *Private Landlords in England*, Occasional Papers in
Social Administration, No. 16 (London: Bell, 1965) and Nevitt, A. A.
Housing, Taxation and Subsidies (London: Nelson, 1966).

accumulated a wide range of powers to regulate and control the privately-rented sector which has grown out of a recognition that this form of tenure is socially and economically indispensable at the present time but that the need to make profits in a declining sector often conflicts with the social and economic resources of those housed by the sector. It hardly needs to be added that privately-rented housing is the only choice for many whose needs are greatest and whose resources are least.

In this chapter we are moving one step closer to the situation of the free market where organizations are profit motivated. We will examine whether agencies with a free market ideology can play a useful role in a comprehensive housing policy. As we shall see there are a wide range of agencies providing such housing, some of which would appear to have a more socially oriented approach. We shall therefore also be examining whether there were particular types of landlords who could more easily be fitted into a comprehensive approach by the authorities or whether the general constraints acting on them were sufficient to make their initial differences of approach insignificant.

We will deal with three distinct groups of agencies: firstly, estate agents who often manage and determine the goals of the smaller landlords; secondly, large company landlords or property companies who are very significant in terms of the numbers of properties they own;[2] and thirdly, two special agencies, the Church Commissioners and the Duchy of Cornwall, who are both large landlords but whose stated goals were rather more complex than the simple pursuit of profit. They are only two of a number of large and old-fashioned institutional or aristocratic landowners which are of particular significance in Inner London.[3]

As in other chapters, in order to see whether the different agencies can play a part in a comprehensive policy we not only

---

[2] The Milner Holland Report showed that whereas over 85 per cent of *landlords* owned less than five properties, and just under 95 per cent less than ten properties, 57 per cent of *properties* were owned by landlords with more than ten properties, and 32 per cent by landlords owning more than 100. Op. cit., p. 317.

[3] These estates include, for instance, the Grosvenor Estate, the Westminster Estate, the Crown Estate Commissioners, Dulwich College, etc.

need to understand the practical effects of their somewhat differing ideologies but also to examine the effect of the constraints they face.

The Aims of the Agencies

The crucial piece of background information is that the privately rented sector is declining for various reasons. The aims of our agencies are concerned with how to survive in the face of this. Let us deal with the estate agents first.

There was a sharp contrast between the Sutton and the Lambeth estate agents in the range of activities available to them. Both the Sutton agents were professionally qualified, i.e. were members of the Royal Institution of Chartered Surveyors (RICS), and clearly had considerable expertise in management, valuation, and the giving of advice to clients on housing, planning, and landlord and tenant law.[4] Both agents were concerned to maximize the return to themselves and their clients from the rented property wherever they could. One agent had encouraged clients to improve their properties if it meant a controlled property becoming decontrolled.[5]

However the two agents thought that the management of rented property would decline as a part of their job, the one feeling this would reflect a fall in demand for this type of property, the other rather that it would be a result of a disproportionate growth in his other agency activities. They would do more management for private developers[6] (collection

---

[4] One managed 600 properties (400 in Sutton) and the other 250 (225 in Sutton). Most of these were unfurnished tenancies—furnished lettings seemed mainly confined to whole houses or flats which, typically, the owners wanted let while they went abroad for a couple of years. The properties they managed were owned by a mixture of small landlords and medium or small companies.

[5] Under the 1969 Housing Act controlled properties can come out of control and be assessed for a 'fair rent' if certain improvements are effected.

[6] One estate agency acted for private developers and bought land for them. Usually this meant buying several houses fit for redevelopment, perhaps with tenants in them who would be offered money to move. The developer would then demolish the house and build a higher density. In

of ground rents, etc.), and professional services (surveys, etc.) would increase. The second one felt also that their interest in commercial property would increase and that individual sales of residential property would probably form a lesser part.

It was evident that there was far less opportunity for diversification of activity in Lambeth where, for example, private development was rare. The one qualified agent we obtained information on[7] concentrated mainly on management and had a highly skilled organization to do this. But the rented stock of housing was fast disappearing in Lambeth and the agent could well be found to have relocated in an area of greater opportunity.

It seemed that it was easier for agents not bound by professional rules and the 'long-term company interest' of the chartered agents to survive in Lambeth in the face of a declining privately-rented sector. For if an agent was willing to handle the kind of property which those on lower incomes depend on, then any attendant problems of rent arrears and evictions were likely to be damaging to the professional firm's long-term interest or public image.

Two of the three 'unqualified' Lambeth agents we spoke to were heavily involved in the furnished lettings market. One of them had been advising landlords to convert to furnished letting as a way of obtaining higher rents. The other had actually been buying up houses, converting them to furnished tenancies for single people, and reselling to other companies, although they had been so dissatisfied with Rent Tribunal

---

fact the estate agency seemed to have a good arrangement all round. It acted for property companies on the one hand, also bought and sold houses, increasing the value in the meantime by removing the tenants, and for developers on the other hand, who were keen on buying the houses ready for redevelopment. The agent earned fees from both ends of the operation. The commission from developers was usually $1\frac{1}{2}$ per cent of the total purchase price, *plus* the fees on the sale of whatever was subsequently built.

[7] We were not able to get direct interviews with either of the two qualified agents we approached in Lambeth. The rest of our discussion of Lambeth's agents is therefore as one-sided as our discussion of Sutton's, but this time relying heavily on the experience of 'unqualified' agents. This is not as bad as it sounds, since so far as we could tell, our selection reflects very much the distribution of agents between the two boroughs as we will indicate later.

decisions that they were now converting houses into unfurnished flats instead.

One agent had also diversified, geographically, out of Lambeth and was concentrating on house sales in Outer London. Another agent had stayed in Lambeth and had devoted his attention to sales but not the kind of sales that members of RICS would necessarily endorse. This agent utilized all financial sources available, so that buyers who were unable to obtain mortgages from the 'normal' source could purchase their own house. They were agents for a medium-sized building society—one of our societies in Chapter Four—and they referred potential purchasers there first of all if they regarded the houses as suitable. The society turned down about half. Then they referred them to the local authority. A quarter of these were unsuccessful. Then they went to a finance company who charged on average an interest rate of 11 per cent—as we described in Chapter Four. They had sold a high proportion of their properties through finance companies and at one time all their business was through them. In fact the agent reckoned that of all the sales they had completed over the past three to four years, 50 per cent of purchasers had used finance companies and the figure got higher in squeeze periods and when there was mortgage rationing. He estimated that during this time they had averaged 150 house sales per annum and that the vast majority of purchasers were coloured. The council's public health inspectors believed that this agent had also been eager to use the generous lending provisions of the GLC mortgage scheme.

Because of the rapid increase in compulsory purchase orders over the last few years, this same agent had cashed in on the fact that property owners have to sell to the local authority, and that the council pays the fees. Agents can circulate any clearance area, and the 'non-professionals' (those who are not members of RICS) can do this quite effectively as the others uphold the professional prohibition on advertising. This agent had completed seventeen such house sales in the preceding twelve months, at £50–£60 per time.

The property companies we looked at had a very different approach. Of course none of the three companies[8] we looked

---

[8] We looked at three property companies. One, based in Sutton, had

at aimed to provide the sorts of services that the 'qualified' or 'unqualified' agents were providing, so their pursuit of profits in the face of a generally declining privately rented sector involved a rather different range of activities.

The two smaller companies were withdrawing from the sector, one far more rapidly than the other. Decisions had been made by the one company twenty years before when it had definitely decided to withdraw from the privately-rented sector as quickly as possible. This Sutton-based company was selling off its rented property and going into commercial development. They had the backing of an insurance company and, as a well-established subsidiary of a development company, this was a natural move to make.

The other company had sold off some houses but was basically holding on to their rented property as it was an appreciating capital asset. However they were not buying more privately-rented accommodation but rather diversifying into commercial renting where rents were determined by free market principles.

However, the company had no intention of breaking up its blocks of flats and selling them off like some other large companies. The reasons behind this provide the key to the maintenance of this part of the privately-rented sector. 'Property is our life blood'. If they sold property they would simply be left with substantial tax liabilities, and the cash is a rapidly depreciating asset. They did not lack means of obtaining cash anyway, so they would prefer to have it in properties bought long ago which were appreciating assets.

The third—and largest—company reacted completely differently. They were acquiring privately-rented blocks in the belief that by obtaining the maximum rent increases allowable under the rent regulation and house improvement system the consequent enhancement of capital values made their continued operation in this sector a profitable activity.

We noted that the 'qualified' estate agents were bound

---

about 580 unfurnished properties in South and West London. The other two were far bigger. One had about 6000 lettings in London and 4000 outside London, and the other 23 000 units, of which 16 000–17 000 were in London. Almost all of these properties were unfurnished flats in purpose-built blocks.

by rules and a particular professional interpretation of their 'long-term company interest' which tended to limit their ability to diversify especially in Lambeth. All three property companies were relatively large concerns and, although not bound by such a professional code, they had to pay some attention to preserving a good reputation in their own interest. Thus it was noticeable that none of them wanted to diversify into furnished rented property and in general to get involved in the lower end of the rented market. Their properties were on the whole well maintained and, apart from the company which was withdrawing from the rented market altogether, they were using improvement grants where appropriate and attempting to convert controlled into regulated tenancies by these means.

In contrast with the agents and the property companies both the Church Commissioners and the Duchy of Cornwall are connected with or accountable to government or 'the establishment' in some way. The Commissioners exist to provide an income to support the clergy and the Duchy performs a similar function for the Prince of Wales. It is evident that some tension will exist between the financial objectives of these two agencies and the expectations of the general public concerning what are and are not appropriate activities for the bodies to be involved in.

The Duchy, which also has extensive rural land holdings, owns an estate (or 'manor') of some 900 properties in Lambeth which are let unfurnished and vary from Georgian houses to modern flats. Until recently the tenancies were let to low-income tenants, either the children of existing tenants or retired royal servants. However, in 1958 the management was contracted out to a firm of estate agents, Daniel Smith, Oakley, and Garrard.[9] As a result a programme of rebuilding and modernization has been embarked on.

The Church Commissioners have also altered their operations since the war. Initially most of their assets were in gilt-edged stock and low-rent, long-lease property. But this policy was abandoned and by 1970 the ordinary shares of commercial and

---

[9] This is one of the old firms of estate agents and surveyors which advised the traditional landowners of London and which figured quite prominently as a link between the old estates, who wanted to modernize and redevelop, and the property barons like Max Rayne, who had the ideas.

industrial companies represented 70 per cent of the book value of the Commissioners' Stock Exchange portfolio. The low-rent, long-lease properties were also sold off and the funds invested in commercial and high-rented residential developments.

The properties that have been disposed of have often gone into development schemes for, as with the Duchy, the main advantage the Commissioners had for building was that they owned the land, even today the commonest form of gift to the Church is land. The investment in other forms of residential and commercial property was facilitated by contacts with developers, initially via Daniel Smith, Oakley and Garrard. By 1966 the property development company founded by the Commissioners, Church Estates Development and Improvement Company, had shared with other developers in twenty-six companies which had started £38.1m of developments (20.7 per cent residential, 79.3 per cent commercial), £20.4m of which were finished.

Thus both the Duchy and the Commissioners have followed the agents and the property companies in actively seeking ways of maintaining and improving the profitability of their business and, in common with most of the other agencies we have looked at, this has involved a move out of privately-rented property into forms of activity which promise a more secure future. By 1970 both the Duchy and the Commissioners had a mixture of higher-rented residential property and low-rented accommodation. Thus one-third of the Kennington manor consists of 'higher-rent' properties (£400–£750 per annum) and the other two-thirds was reserved for the traditional categories of tenants for children of existing tenants and for transfers and decants.

To some extent both agencies regard the maintenance of this proportion of low-income housing in their stock as a justification of their view that they do exercise a fair measure of social concern despite their primary duty to maximize the income of their main beneficiaries. We shall illustrate the scope and limitations of this attitude.

Although the Rent Acts have not applied to the Duchy, it has still tended to apply them unofficially. Until the modernization programme began, the rents of the older properties had been fixed at controlled rent levels, but as they fell vacant 'fair rents' were fixed, unless the tenant could not afford the new rent in which case it would be adjusted accordingly.

It was also hoped that prospective tenants would work in the South London area, because the Duchy wanted to encourage a sense of 'community'. This was a very large area however and seemed to have stretched as letting policy had changed (e.g. it came to include the City for the higher-rented properties) and since the late fifties they have housed people who were not locally employed at all. In addition the Duchy wanted to retain the objective of social mixing. Again the goal appeared to have arisen mainly because of the change in letting policy, it being difficult to retain the old objective of letting to the working class if the rents of new properties are between £5 and £15 per week.

The Church Commissioners also wanted to modernize properties and get 'fair rents' assessed but they had also managed to produce new dwelling units for lower-income groups. By the end of 1971 they had 1000 flats in Lambeth, the most recent addition being 271 new flats built by the Commissioners acting as a housing association. The scheme in Lambeth was the largest housing association scheme undertaken by the Commissioners. However the scheme could only have yielded a return of 1–2 per cent if the Commissioners had used their own capital in the scheme, and they would not have proceeded with it on this basis. By using their housing association status, they were entitled to Exchequer subsidies and a GLC rate fund contribution. In return the GLC nominated all the tenants. The First Estates Commissioner thought that the local authority was the rightful agency for doing this low-income development. In other words the aims of the Commissioners were very strongly geared to maximizing the income of the clergy, despite claims by some clergymen that they should provide for the poor too.

Thus all the agencies reacted to the declining fortunes of the privately-rented sector by diversifying out of this sector and/or by altering the nature of their operations within it. The response to this situation varied with the way in which the agencies thought it possible to maintain the need for profits in the light of their conception of their 'long-term company interest'.

For one reason or another most of the agencies have still got some privately-rented stock. Either 'property is their life blood' or they thought it an appreciating asset, or if they managed the property as estate agents they were increasing the income by recommending the use of improvement grants despite diversifying into other activities at the same time. The two 'old estates' had retained some rented properties for 'social reasons' and had otherwise invested in higher-income rented property.

In the next section we will examine the constraints these agencies faced in retaining privately-rented property and we will then be able to discuss the kinds of people the agencies housed.

The Constraints They Faced

Broadly speaking the agencies we are concerned with in this chapter face three sets of constraints although not all of these are equally significant for the different agencies. The constraints are:

1 The controls and regulations on the privately-rented sector exerted by central and local government.
2 Obligations towards those to whom the agencies are mainly accountable and the limitations they place on the agencies' operations.
3 The part of the market in which the agencies operate, both in geographic and socio-economic terms.

Furthermore these are not completely independent of each other. For example, the constraints imposed by government regulation may endorse or conflict with the limitations imposed on an agency because of the part of the market in which it is operating. The basic point to be made is that all the agencies we have described above need to make profits, whether for themselves, their clients, landlords, shareholders, the clergy, or the Prince of Wales and the success with which they are able to do so via rented property depends on the ability they have to negotiate the limitations imposed by these constraints.

Central government legislation affecting the privately-rented sector was potentially the most general constraint affecting all the agencies. Broadly speaking this has aimed at establishing norms of equity between landlord and tenant and trying to ensure that, at a minimum, property is maintained in a state where it is fit and safe for human habitation, and more positively is improved so as to prevent the accelerating physical decay of the privately-rented sector. The legislation ranges from simple controls, e.g. to prevent overcrowding and multiple occupation and ensure proper management and repair of accommodation, to attempts to upgrade the stock over whole areas, e.g. improvement grants and General Improvement Areas.[10] Apart from this legislation concerned with the quality of the stock and physical conditions within it the various Rent Acts, recently reviewed by the Francis Committee [1], are concerned to provide reasonable rents, a measure of security of tenure for tenants, and freedom from harassment.

The codes which govern these matters in the furnished and the unfurnished sector are different. The 1965 (later 1968) Rent Act set up a system of Rent Officers and Rent Assessment Panels to determine 'fair rents' and deal with matters affecting security of tenure in the unfurnished sector whereas the older established Rent Tribunals set rents and security in the furnished sector. On the whole the provisions are more favourable to unfurnished than furnished tenants both with respect to rent levels and security. Various criticisms have been made of the variations between the codes, of their general ineffectiveness and of the way in which it is the landlords rather than the tenants which have made most use of the legislation [2] and [3].

Another factor affecting the agencies' freedom of operation is their accountability. Here there are no general rules. The differences between the agencies in this respect will emerge as we discuss them below.

Finally the market position of the agencies affects their operations differentially. In general agencies which operate in areas with better quality property are also able to let to tenants in higher socio-economic categories (and this is mainly unfurnished letting). Here the problems are less than in areas where the reverse is true and although it is not necessarily the case that profits are higher in areas of better quality property, the agencies are more easily able to avoid severe difficulties in these areas. No hard-and-fast distinction can be made between Sutton and Lambeth on this dimension but it tends to be the case that the

---

[10] Much of this legislation is contained in the 1957, 1961, 1964, and 1969 Housing Acts. The bulk of this legislation is exercised by various local authority departments or sections especially those staffed by the housing, public health, and planning professions.

Lambeth agencies were operating towards the bottom, i.e. furnished, end of the market where the problems imposed by all three sets of constraints and their interactions were greater than in Sutton.

Let us examine first of all how these three constraints affected the estate agents and the rented property they managed or owned.

We saw that one of the Sutton agents encouraged owners to use improvement grants, but generally the Sutton agents argued that the 'fair rents' fixed by the Rent Officer were not sufficient to provide a reasonable return on the property owners' capital even when the house was improved and higher rents could be charged. Despite the increase in rents due to improvement they felt that the 1969 Act was definitely not enough to make people continue to rent rather than sell and sometimes they would suggest to the landlords whose properties they managed that selling the property would probably be a better course of action. Both Sutton agents also found it annoying that Rent Officer decisions varied so much between boroughs.

However in Sutton the agents did at least have some success in using the Rent Officer system and getting rents increased after improvements to the properties were effected. Firstly, the houses were generally in reasonable condition to start with. Secondly, the owners to whom the agents were accountable often had sufficient resources to meet their part of the cost of improvements and repairs. Thirdly, the Sutton tenants themselves tended to be able to afford the revised rents and were often willing to have the improvements carried out.

The Lambeth agents faced a different situation altogether. Firstly, the property they handled was in a poorer condition than in Sutton and secondly, both owners and tenants had fewer resources. Many properties were still in control but it was particularly difficult to interest owners in improvements to bring them out of control because the 'fair rents' which would then be assessed would not justify the effort on such older property, even if they could afford to improve them. Because of the condition of the properties the agents managed, many had also been scheduled for demolition by the local authority in the near future so making any improvements impracticable. Finally, many tenants were very poor or objected to improvements[11] so the improvement of property was a non-starter for this reason too.

Managing or owning poorer rented property in the inner area also meant that the agents or owners were embroiled with the local authority in its attempts to regulate and control conditions. The one professional agent we got information about in Lambeth was doing a useful job transmitting the local authority's demands to his clients and trying to persuade them to improve conditions, or reduce multiple occupation. But in the situation in Lambeth where neither landlords nor tenants were able to afford much, this tended to be an unprofitable activity. Unlike his competitors in Lambeth, the agent's professional code forbade resort to many of the more dubious ways in which the other agents managed to diversify their activities or get round the constraints in the rented sector.

The Lambeth 'unqualified' agent who had largely moved his activities out of Lambeth still managed some property in the better parts of the borough. He specifically limited the range of landlords he was prepared to manage for because of the local authority controls. Managing properties for the landlords of poorer property which the authority was trying to regulate did not pay a higher commission so the extra effort of acting on the landlord's behalf was not worth it. Where the council had actually threatened to take action against the agent in its management role, this estate agency's practice had been to reply that they were no longer the agents or that they would relinquish any responsibility for the property if the landlord did not comply immediately. Again if the landlord wanted vacant possession they would not serve a notice to quit on the landlord's behalf. He had to do it himself.

One agent had attempted to avoid the controls of the Rent Officer and the local authority by managing and owning furnished property and improving it. He made his money by managing for subsidiary companies he owned, buying, improving, and selling the properties between companies, raising the cash through mortgages from finance companies, and

---

[11] Under Section 55 of the 1969 Housing Act, a Court Order to install improvements if a tenant objects does not apply if the tenant has an income which would qualify him/her for a rate rebate.

collecting the fees (which are tax deductible). Or in some cases he would sell the improved property to owner occupiers or landlords. Lambeth's public health inspectors alleged that the agent had tried to get them to issue overcrowding orders or use similar means to remove controlled tenants and others who were generally disliked because they were depressing the value of property, preventing conversions, or requiring money to be spent on repairs. The inspectors also alleged that a member of the council had been used by the agent to obtain improvement grants. The agent was sure that this member had influence and was using it on his behalf. The agent complained quite bitterly of how the inspectors seemed to be persecuting him—issuing notices and orders at the slightest provocation and insisting on the most expensive equipment when improvements were in progress. In one dispute the agent had sent the relevant papers to the member he had contact with and no more had been heard. There was obviously such a great deal of bitterness between the inspectors and the agent in this attempt to impose or avoid controls that it was hard to tell what was going on. The agent stated that he had got rid of his subsidiary companies anyway because of the liabilities incurred through corporation tax. But various loopholes exist to enable such an agent to minimize tax liabilities by having subsidiary companies, buying up property on mortgages so as to always appear in debt and avoid corporation tax, and then selling to other subsidiaries or owner occupiers thus incurring capital gains tax—much less than corporation tax. The fact that this agent was called by one name, leases were signed on the forms of a company with another, and the name on the door of the offices was yet another suggested that this might well have been going on.

This devious attempt to survive in the face of regulations and controls provides a good example of how some property is staying in the privately-rented sector, being upgraded, and converted to furnished tenancies. Otherwise estate agents, and this agent too to a certain extent, have given the decline of the privately-rented sector a further push because of the additional constraints they face. They have done this because management incurs problems due to pressures and controls from the local authority particularly in the inner areas, because the Rent Officer does not provide a sufficient return for landlords, and because there are other activities they can turn to in order to maximize fees. It is not difficult to see how the effect of the Rent Officer has made management insecure for agents and why the agents should recommend that properties be sold, or at least converted to furnished lettings. Legislation has encouraged landlords to improve properties and get properties out of control and agents generally support this although there is a significant reluctance to take any active part because of the staff time that would have to be devoted to something which is a rapidly declining part of their total activity. There are differences of course, especially between those in Lambeth and those in Sutton, the latter not being so outspoken about which activities they disliked. This reflects the lack of pressure and the wider diversity of alternatives that the professionally qualified agent can turn to which is more apparent in Outer than Inner London. So overall, legislative controls have been additional factors which have nudged estate agents into finding new roles, some increasing their professional and survey work perhaps quite unconsciously as demand for it rises, and some struggling to find a niche in areas of rapid change and to preserve professional respectability at the same time. Others have been drifting quite easily into fields which capitalize on the declining rented sector and the difficulty for certain groups of getting somewhere secure to rent, by increasing the amount of furnished accommodation where evictions are easier to obtain, by improving property they own and selling it off, or by selling houses via finance company mortgages.

All three property companies were similar to the Sutton agents in catering more for the upper end of the rented market and letting mainly unfurnished property. As with the Sutton agents the property was usually in sound condition and the problems created by local authority intervention were minimal. The main constraints on the companies seemed to have arisen out of a combination of the effect of the system of rent regulation and their shareholders' or owners' evaluation of the prospects given the continuance of this system in the future. Each of the companies reacted differently to these problems.

The Sutton company had not had to improve their properties much in order to qualify for a 'fair rent' under the 1969 Housing Act because the houses were quite modern. But the rent regulation system was seen as one further reason for getting out of rented property.

The second company provides the best example of the financial constraints facing a public company with rented property. Its main priority was to maintain the rate of dividend to the shareholders and to increase it whenever possible. Therefore the shareholders had to be considered in everything the company did in order to maintain the status of the company as an investment medium. Properties could not remain empty for any period of time as this affected profitability and thereby the dividend. This company's dividends have moved steadily upwards in recent years. Financing of operations had relied on long-term borrowing on the strength of existing properties, although with rising interest rates over the past few years they had switched to short-term borrowing. This meant that profits were not retained to finance operations but were distributed as dividends.

These financial constraints made the purchase of any more rented property a non-starter. In the fifties and early sixties, when interest rates were relatively low, they could borrow at 6 per cent and then make a much higher return on property. This meant that property companies grew quite fast in this period. However now the company could not obtain anything like the 10 per cent return they required with the level of rents set by the Rent Officers and Assessment Committees.

The retention of rented property, as opposed to buying more of it, in the face of the rent regulation system, had the effect of depressing share prices below their 'true' value. This had two consequences. Firstly, dividends had to be maintained and increased (the lower the share price, the higher the dividend necessary to retain investment and confidence). Secondly, a public company like this one, which was growing by diversifying and buying other companies, had to give out a disproportionate number of its shares in exchange for those of other companies in many takeover bids. It would not have had to have done this if the share price was at its 'true' value.

Rented property thus created a number of difficulties in terms of the accountability the company had to its shareholders (as expressed through the workings of the market, as with building societies, rather than via the Annual General Meeting). For these reasons the company definitely thought that if they retained privately-rented property for much longer they might ultimately lose out. But they gambled on the Rent Officer and regulation system being changed some time in the future to allow landlords more profit. This in fact might happen with 'agreed rents' under the 1972 Housing Finance Act. But the company saw that if in the long run they did not get a better return from residential property they should get out of it and their increasing concentration on the acquisition of com- mercial property over the last three to four years was a reaction to this situation.

Unlike the company just described, the third company has embarked on a policy of large-scale acquisition of privately- rented properties and this has occurred for the most part *since* the 1965 Rent Act. Between 1968 and 1971 the assets of the company doubled from £50m to £100m and although much of the new acquisition was commercial property, 60 per cent of the stock in 1971 was residential. Along with this expansion the company instituted a series of measures including a tenant welfare service, a house magazine, and special help in cases of hardship. It explained that these were aimed at removing the distrust people have of landlords and also offering those among them who could afford to buy a house something they would value as much as this asset.

Together with these practices went a skilful approach to negotiating the constraints imposed by the 1965 Rent Act. This involved the realization that this Act gave the landlord the right to apply for a rent increase every three years—compared with a period of seven, sixteen, or twenty-one years in most commercial property leases. Given this the company looked for blocks of flats with artificially low rents, in which it was easiest to increase the rents. They would try to buy from insurance companies among others who had often hung on to older blocks without pushing rents up because they were afraid of blemishing their public image. This had two advantages. Because of their low income the price at which they were sold often made them a bargain. Also the institutions were keen to sell to someone who would not break up and sell off the pro- perties but continue to manage them thus avoiding bad publicity.

When a letting became vacant the company would ask the new tenant to sign a 'joint application' to the Rent Officer asking for the agreed rent, usually the market rent, to be registered as the 'fair rent'. Sometimes the tenant would be asked to sign a blank form—the rent was filled in later. It would be difficult for a tenant hard up for somewhere to live and faced with a steadily declining stock of privately-rented properties to refuse to sign. Rent Officers would be impressed by a joint application, since it was explicitly stated in the House of Commons that 'the first emphasis of rent regulation under the Bill is on agreement between the landlord and tenant'.[12] So a joint application might carry more weight than just a tenant or landlord application, particularly since the 'scarcity element' which is supposed to be excluded in aiming at a 'fair rent' is difficult to define in any calculation of the most equitable rent.

Frequently Rent Officers' decisions would be taken to appeal since even one successful appeal on, for example, a block of flats establishes a precedent which is used by the Rent Officer to determine all the other rents in the block. Obviously only a large landlord with considerable resources can afford to pursue this course of action. Finally, even where there was a registered rent for a dwelling, the company tried to get an increase from a new tenant should a flat become vacant. A tenant can only claim up to two years payments of excess by civil action, he cannot sue the landlord, and the landlord is committing no criminal offence. The company considered that the absence of legal penalties for charging a market rent, even when the property in question had a registered rent, could only have been intentional. Evidence that we collected from Rent Officers confirmed that this was going on. Viewed in this light this company's attempts to promote the image of a humane and socially oriented landlord, while doubtless of value in itself can be seen to have another important function for the company by reducing the likelihood that tenants would object to signing joint agreements, paying agreed rather than 'fair' rents and co-operating in the attempt to gain the maximum rent increases possible.

The whole point of the operation was to raise the capital

---

[12] *House of Commons Debates*, 5 July, 1965, Col. 1138. Joint Parliamentary Secretary to the Minister of Housing and Local Government, in third reading of Rent Bill.

values of the property (which are a multiple of rental income) and thus increase the assets of the company. With the aid of the increased value of a block a new and higher mortgage could be raised on it and further property bought. In this the company, unlike the previous one we discussed, is at a considerable advantage in not being a public company. The company maintains that property is a long/medium-term investment and public companies are tied to half-yearly reports to shareholders. Some properties which look good in the long run look poor in the short run and having to announce this kind of thing every six months causes share prices to fluctuate wildly. By being private they can buy cheap blocks, improve them slowly, leave large numbers empty while they do so, and eventually revalue them. The mortgages give the appearance of making a loss and no corporation tax is payable. When the properties are sold, if at all, the assets are subject to capital gains tax which as we have already stated is far less than corporation tax.

It may be other companies are beginning to initiate this strategy. We were told that the other large company we studied was moving in this direction, although it would obviously be constrained in certain respects by its public status. In any event there are clearly good reasons why the large company landlord has not declined as rapidly as others. But another constraint has arisen for companies which are catering for the upper-income groups. By pressing for as much rental income as possible they have stimulated the growth of articulate tenants' associations. One of the companies in particular had experienced the effects of these associations objecting to their practices, claiming back excess rent and making bad publicity. However in a situation where there is an acute shortage of rented accommodation there must be severe limitations to the effectiveness of these protests.

Property companies have thus reacted rather differently from the estate agents to government controls. Some have actively tried to use the rent regulation system to their own advantage and others at the very least have decided to hold on to their properties for the time being because of the advantages it potentially offers. This is partly because they had better property to begin with, partly because they saw loopholes in the legislation, but partly also because, despite their public protestations to the contrary, they saw Rent Officer decisions working in their favour. It is worth looking at this last point a little more closely.

The Rent Assessment Panel has circulated Rent Officers with examples of decisions so that their assessments would not vary too much from borough to borough. We found that Rent Officers did look to these decisions to provide a larger context for their own assessments. But the average percentage change made by Rent Assessment Committees in London in 1969 was to increase by 4 per cent the rent which the Rent Officer had assessed. Of 875 appeals dealt with 47.7 per cent were increases on the Rent Officers' determination, 37.9 per cent were no change, and only 14.3 per cent decreases [4]. Finally the rate of landlord applications to the Rent Officer has gone up significantly since 1966, but the rate of appeals (in London) has gone down drastically, probably reflecting the upward revision of assessments by Rent Officers and landlords' reactions to this.[13]

Our work showed that the large landlords were the largest single source of application (47 per cent in Lambeth and 34 per cent in Sutton).[14] Furthermore, among the large landlords it was the biggest—especially the two we interviewed—who were using the mechanism most, especially in Lambeth where there were more large landlords anyway.

It is quite understandable that the larger landlords should be the first off the mark in applying to the Rent Officers and that they should take advantage of the upward trends in rents which have been encouraged by the Rent Assessment Panel. They are the ones whose 'life blood is property', who would have to consider selling off more properties if the system were not revised in their favour—because of the strong financial and commercial constraints involved in a large public company intent on retaining confidence and investment.

Like the property companies both the Church Commissioners and the Duchy of Cornwall had managed to avoid many of the problems that beset the smaller landlords and their agents. Their property was in good condition and there was no shortage of money to keep it so. Obviously then they rarely had diffi-

---

[13] Poor tenants in particular have not been applying for reductions under the Rent Acts. See Zander [2] and Donnison [3].
[14] See Appendix for details of samples.

culties arising from legislation concerned with the maintenance
of adequate standards.

Furthermore apart from the overall need to obtain a secure
and rising income from the property, there were no obvious
bodies to whom they were directly accountable and who were
likely to insist on maximum returns regardless of circumstances.
On the other hand there was also no one to whom they were
directly responsible for any social justification for their actions.[15]
The main, but hardly major, constraint was the increase in
tenant association activity. In 1971, forty tenants on a new,
higher-rented, estate were given an ultimatum about proposed
rent increases which would almost double some rents. Representatives of the Commissioners met a delegation of tenants and
told them that as a charity they were obliged to earn as much
as they could and that no reductions could be considered. Most
of the one- and two-bedroomed flats effected had a rateable
value of less than £400 and were therefore subject to the Rent
Acts. But the leader of the tenants' association was of the
opinion that this was of little help since landlords could submit
as evidence the fact that other people were paying rents similar
to the increases being applied for. For the association the
difficulty was that the Commissioners had been able to get
commercial tenants to sign new agreements—therefore demon-
strating that the 'true' market rents were higher than those
current—since these tenants have little personal stake in the

---

[15] Apart from three honorary officers, the Prince of Wales (or the Monarch
if he is not of age) appoints members who live in the area in which the
Duchy has property, or whose opinions will be valuable in managing that
property. Accounts are submitted to Parliament, but the Duchy is not
actually accountable to Parliament, apart from a provision which requires
Treasury approval for a warrant for capital expenditure.

Of the ninety-five Church Commissioners at the time of our work, forty-
two were diocesan bishops, and most of the rest were elected by the
General Synod of the Church. In addition, four were appointed by the
Queen (on the advice of the Prime Minister), and four by the Archbishop
of Canterbury. There were also some lay members including a local
government administrator, a solicitor, a bank manager, merchant
bankers, and the president of an insurance company. The role of the
First Estates Commissioner is to 'form the link between Church and
State', but the formal link with the State is by way of the Second Estates
Commissioner, who answers questions in the House. His position is a
political appointment once described as—'the last appointment made by
an incoming Prime Minister, and the lowest form of Ministerial life'.

rent and in addition they are unlikely to identify with the goals of a tenants' association.

Other constraints have arisen because of the shortage of dwellings into which to 'decant' tenants during improvements. Thus, for example, applicants for the Duchy's lower-income properties could only be housed after an average wait of four years owing to the fact that many vacancies were required for those tenants affected by improvement operations. Improvements often slowed down in any case because of the shortage of alternative dwellings.

However in general the Church Commissioners and the Duchy, in company with the large landlords, had managed to negotiate the constraints of accountability and rent regulation rather successfully. The older 'estates' and the property companies had not been affected by the attempts of local authorities to control conditions in the privately-rented sector because of the better condition of property, the greater resources of landlord and tenant, and the active use of 'loopholes' in the Rent Acts.

As a result of our examination of these aims and constraints, what can we learn of their effect on the type of tenants housed?

Who the Agencies Housed

The estate agencies saw their continuation in the privately-rented sector as a second-best solution so far as profit maximization for themselves and their clients was concerned. To the extent that they stayed in this business they tried to minimize management problems and to avoid the direct controls of the local authority over factors such as multiple occupation and disrepair.

So the agents were quite selective in their choice of tenants to avoid problems of non-payment of rent, disturbances caused by children, and general maltreatment of property. Even the estate agent who was actively converting his tenancies to furnished accommodation was imposing stricter eligibility criteria in his tenant selection process. Thus in a declining stock, helped on its way by estate agents in many cases, that is becoming more furnished, it is becoming increasingly difficult for people, families with children in particular, to obtain a reasonable and secure tenancy.

This is borne out by the activities of the older 'estates' and the property companies. Their 'long-term company interest' and their desire to avoid the expense attached to management problems means that they asked for bank and employer references from prospective clients, that they generally did not want children in their flats (with one exception), and that they had strict income requirements—in one company a family with two children was required to earn £30 a week in order to pay £4 rent.

The Duchy and the Commissioners were steadily recruiting a higher social class of tenant as a result of their modernization and new building programmes and the accompanying higher rents. Here as with the property companies the change in clientele has been less the product of regulation and controls than the pursuit of more revenue *per se*. But, unlike the companies, the estates do not have the far stricter constraints of financial accountability that require that property must remain a good, stable, untarnished investment medium. So, despite their aura of social responsibility, the older estates appear to be the one group of the three main types of agency we have looked at in this chapter who are becoming less inclined to take lower-income groups solely because of the pursuit of increased revenue rather than because of the limitations imposed by constraints.

In the Duchy the tenants of the old properties were usually elderly themselves, and included market workers, postmen, and clerks. But as a result of the new building and modernization and the need to look further afield than the local 'community' for tenants to pay the higher rents, the newer tenants ranged from teachers and nurses to Members of Parliament. The socio-economic distribution was still biased towards the lower half of the spectrum but it was gradually extending into the white-collar/professional/managerial grades.

In addition, in so far as lower-income people were concerned, these estates and the property companies were largely 'closed shops'. Most new tenants at this income level were recommended by existing tenants and this proved to be quite a successful system for the organizations involved. They rarely advertised their vacancies, only doing so in the event of a higher-rented dwelling not being quickly taken up.

The one company we managed to collect data from highlights some of these factors.[16] Sixty-three per cent of the households had no children and another 23 per cent had one (there was no information for 10 per cent). Total family size was therefore low. Over 80 per cent of the households consisted of three persons or less. Unfortunately we could collect no data on age and marital status. The companies' own survey of tenants showed that 51 per cent were over 50, 21 per cent between 35 and 50, and 22 per cent under 35. We also know that none of our sample was retired.

The occupational distribution of tenants was concentrated in the upper socio-economic groups although the groupings were much more evenly distributed in Outer London. But the greatest difference in both Inner and Outer London between the company's tenants on the one hand and the borough's on the other was in the managerial and professional groups.[17] This general concentration in the middle and upper grades appeared in the income figures too[18] and was naturally reflected in the rents people paid.[19]

Thus the picture that emerged of this company's tenants is one of a group of white-collar, professional/managerial people, with no children, either just starting family life or the older type of childless professional family. They are particularly suited to what Inner London can offer, they do not have to move out to the suburbs, and those that do live further out do so because they are less able to afford Inner London rents.

---

[16] See Appendix for details of the weakness of the sample.

[17] In Lambeth 45·3 per cent of the companies' tenants were in the managerial and professional groups and 47·6 per cent in the nonmanual group compared with figures of 11·6 per cent and 24 per cent respectively for the borough as a whole. The company had no unskilled or semi-skilled service tenants and few skilled workers.

In Sutton/Bromley (see Appendix on Methodology) there were 40·7 per cent in the managerial and professional groups compared with 25·5 per cent in the boroughs as a whole. The proportion of skilled and nonmanual workers was fairly close to the average but once again there were no unskilled tenants and only 3·7 per cent semi-skilled service tenants, compared with the overall average of 10·2 per cent in the two boroughs.

[18] Mean income for all tenants in the sample was £39 per week, higher in Lambeth and lower in Sutton/Bromley.

[19] Only one tenant in each of the two samples paid less than £7·50 per week. 36 per cent of the Lambeth sample paid £10 or more per week and 22 per cent in Sutton/Bromley.

These characteristics must reflect to an ever-increasing extent the type of tenant housed by companies, the older estates, and estate agents, for different reasons. What hope is there then of a local authority involving the privately-rented sector in a comprehensive housing policy? Our evidence will show that the local authority has to rely on the kind of landlord who is catering for the people who are being turned down by the increasingly restrictive nature of these organizations' activities.

The Limitations of a Comprehensive Housing Policy

The discussion of the intervention of the local authorities in the privately-rented sector and the implications for a comprehensive housing policy will mainly concern itself with the Lambeth situation, for both Sutton council and the GLC have not chosen to intervene in this sector to any great extent.

The GLC, as we mentioned in the Introduction, does not have the public health powers which other councils use to combat multiple occupation. But after 1969 it could have declared General Improvement Areas. However it only declared its first such area after our study was completed as a result of increasing pressure on it to give more assistance to Inner London. Shortly before this declaration it also proposed a general compulsory purchase order for the selective redevelopment and rehabilitation of private property in another area.

In Sutton rented accommodation on the whole was in reasonable condition and the high level of housing stress found in Lambeth did not exist. The decline of the privately-rented sector did not present a local authority which was concerned to ensure that some provision was made for all needs with the same problems as Lambeth and the local authority was rarely involved in the use of its public health and housing powers to control and ameliorate poor conditions.[20] In Sutton the two areas of need where the council had decided that most help was required were the elderly and the marginal owner occupier and we have seen how, in their policy towards housing associations and their own mortgage scheme, they had taken steps to achieve these aims. To the extent that Sutton enabled people to

---

[20] See GLC, *Annual Abstract of Greater London Statistics*, 1967–69.

buy or find an association tenancy, they were enabling the run down of the privately-rented sector to take place in their borough with less stress than otherwise might occur. But the main point is that the imbalance between the supply of rented accommodation and the demand for it was not so great as to cause serious problems.

In Lambeth the situation was altogether different. The problem was that, while the privately-rented sector had declined due to landlords selling out and the council redeveloping large areas, the demand for this accommodation was not declining so fast. The property was also generally in a poor state, and was being let increasingly in furnished and more insecure tenancies. So the level of stress was high. Furthermore the majority of the landlords did not have the resources to upgrade their property. Neither would the majority of the tenants have had sufficient incomes to meet the higher rents that would then have prevailed.

Therefore the local authority faced a complex and difficult situation. Firstly, the rented sector served a section of need which, because of its sheer size, could not in the foreseeable future be catered for by the public or housing association sectors. Therefore attempts had to be made, at the very least, to slow down its numerical decline. On the other hand while such a view might, and did, lead to a policy of co-operation with landlords, it was the duty of the authority to control and regulate the worst excesses of the sector by using the powers vested in it and this sometimes involved the use of coercion rather than co-operation. Finally, since large parts of the rented sector were decaying and the authority wished to stop the decline by persuading landlords to improve their property, the problem of lack of resources came to the fore.

Earlier we outlined the structure of Lambeth's Housing Directorate, and explained how it included public health inspectors, a Housing Advice Centre, and how the Advice Centre was the front-line medium between, on the one hand, all the agencies Lambeth wanted to involve in its strategy, and on the other, the co-ordinated Department and its staff. In addition the borough had started to tackle the problem of sharing and lack of amenities by introducing a register of houses in multiple occupation, and was intending to improve the quality of the environment and housing amenities in general by embarking on an extensive General Improvement Area programme.[21] The council was trying to co-operate with landlords as well as regulate them and their agents and, through the medium of the Advice Centre, it was trying to change the whole 'public health' tradition. It believed that landlords should be invited to form links with the borough to establish mutual interests rather than be abated as nuisances.

These arrangements were only part of a more general approach to landlords. When a landlord was willing to improve his property to the required standard, in suitable cases, the council offered to rehouse the tenants in order that the necessary works could be carried out. The landlord then had to accept council nominees as his new tenants but he could choose from a list of nominated tenants and, if he later regretted his choice, the council would rehouse the tenants concerned and offer another list. The landlord was encouraged to use this procedure as a means of avoiding the phasing of rent increases required by the conversion of controlled tenancies to 'fair rent' level. A new tenancy means that the 'fair rent' can be charged straightaway. Until a system of housing allowances for private tenants was proposed by central government the borough only nominated people whose rent was paid by the Supplementary Benefits Commission or who were otherwise able to afford the new 'fair rent'. The council got the borough's housing stock improved, and the landlord maximized his income.

Finally, the council attempted to improve housing conditions in the borough by encouraging a permanent reduction in the resident population. The registration scheme enabled the borough to control the spread of multiple occupation in its area[22] and prevent poor conditions from getting worse but it had a more positive aspect because it was hoped that the health inspectors and their assistants would actually be able to per-

---

[21] Under Part II of the 1969 Housing Act.

[22] Multiple occupation was seen increasingly as a problem of the whole borough. Houses in Streatham in the South, which had a relative absence of housing stress contained houses which were being subdivided into as many as fourteen lettings, according to the public health inspectors. In the past the lettings were occupied by young professionals but more recently the Department had evidence of working-class families moving into the area.

suade the landlords to improve and upgrade their property at the same time. The scheme therefore contained elements of coercion and co-operation.

To cover the whole borough effectively required a large increase in the public health inspectorate and this problem was met by the introduction of technical assistants. The assistants' job was solely one of inspection and registration of properties. However, they did perform a crucial negotiating role when it came to explaining to the landlord or his agent in the course of registration what action would be taken under the Housing Acts and what the council was offering by way of grants and loans.

Nevertheless staffing did impose constraints. The problem of shortage of staff meant that the sections requiring the actual provision of amenities or for default work to be arranged and supervised (Section 14, 15, and 18 of the 1961 Act and the Control Order provision of the 1964 Act) received less than equal emphasis in the control of multiple occupation. Sections 14 and 15 which were used less by Lambeth than some other boroughs are the main powers for ensuring that anything gets done in the provision of amenities and repair work. Sections 12 and 19 by themselves do not guarantee anything—the one empowers an authority to apply a 'management code', the other allows the authority to issue a direction order fixing a limit to occupancy levels but not enforcing any reduction until the landlords relets a part, or the whole of the dwelling. The heavy concentration on registration schemes and the collection of information about the extent of multiple occupation could well have detracted resources and staff from the application of the other sections.

Another problem was created by the legislation which often places the burden of proof too heavily on the local authority or involves them in enormous responsibilities. For example regular detailed inspections are required in order to enforce orders, and heavy rehousing commitments or large and often unrecoverable outlays for works in default are involved. In drafting the legislation Parliament has been especially careful that the rights of property ownership are not excessively infringed and in the view of the Lambeth public health inspectorate many of the regulations were 'long-winded, cautious, and weak'.

The main problem however concerned the fact that the bulk of the property and conditions that Lambeth were dealing with were those at the bottom end of the market where the situation was at its worst and most work needed to be done. On the other hand it was just the landlords of this property who were most unable or unwilling to accede to Lambeth's co-operative or coercive policies. These were of course small landlords who, as we have seen, were often represented by the unqualified agents.

Various analyses of the Lambeth register of multiple occupation confirm that the smaller landlord was mainly involved. Sixty-one per cent of the landlords on the register either lived at the same address as the registered property or lived elsewhere in Lambeth and owned less than ten properties in the borough. Furthermore 59 per cent of all notices served under the Housing Acts to control and ameliorate conditions in houses in multiple occupation involved these two categories of landlord. Large company landlords did not figure at all. In fact the organizations in the large landlords/agents category who had notices served on them were eight estate agents. The two whose names appeared most often in this category were two of the three unqualified agents we referred to earlier— the one selling houses via finance company mortgages and the other doing conversion into furnished flatlets. But even the qualified agent we obtained information on figured highly in this section, thus confirming the difficulties he faced in the Lambeth situation.

Our analysis underlined the difficulty that many of these owner occupier landlords and small landlords might have in financing improvements and co-operating with the council's strategy. Eighty-eight of the 562 properties registered as being in multi-occupation were recorded as mortgaged. Forty-three of these had the landlord living on the premises and twenty-three living elsewhere in the borough. Only 37 per cent of the eighty-eight mortgages were from a building society. The rest were from various sources including banks (10 per cent), finance companies (17 per cent) and others including private individuals (21 per cent). In other words, there was a significant relationship for the smaller landlord between multiple occupation and mortgages from unconventional lending agencies. This may have been because the landlord had no alternative source of housing himself because of discrimination if he was black, or other constraints he faced [5], or because he wanted to 'bleed' the property as an absentee landlord (lots of tenants, high rents, having to borrow from a non-conventional source), or because he wanted to be an owner occupier for its own sake and disliked being in debt for long periods.[23] Whichever it was the higher repayments that he often incurred (especially from finance companies, as we described in Chapter Two) to pay off quite highly-priced houses in Inner London meant that he had to take on as many tenants as he could.

It is extremely unlikely that the landlord paying off an extortionate mortgage, or at least relatively high interest payments, will be able to improve, will be willing to co-operate in terms of reducing the occupancy level of his property, or will be attracted by the offer of having tenants rehoused so as to improve the property and increase the rent. It is likely to be as high as possible already and the property is often let on a furnished basis so that the advantage of avoiding the 'fair rent' phasing does not exist.

If this is the type of property with the highest rent (in relation to income of tenants) it is also the type of property with the most friction between landlord and tenant, where improvement is not the only problem. We noticed in applications to the Rent Officer that the most active were the large landlords and that resident landlords did not figure very much (43 out of 805 applications in Lambeth came from landlords or their tenants and 28 of these were landlords or joint landlord/tenant applications). In applications to the Rent Tribunal however, 67 per cent of applications were from tenants sharing their accommodation with their landlord. The applications were either for a reduction in rent or security of tenure, or both.[24] The Clerk to the Tribunal thought that often the landlord had issued a notice to quit because he was selling out when he realized the cost of the repayments he had to make or when the payments got unrealistically high. In these cases, the

---

[23] This seems more likely to be the explanation in areas of non-stress. Compare Gower Davies, J. *The Evangelistic Bureaucrat* (London: Tavistock, 1971).

[24] Compared to Sutton where the applications were more likely to be for a reduction in rent than for security of tenure.

landlord would prefer to be able to sell the house with vacant possession.

These conditions of friction in which the landlord wants the highest rent, where the tenants are crammed in and threatened with eviction if the local authority tries to get evidence about contravention of direction orders, are not the most conducive to co-operation. Unless the local authority could rehouse the tenants, renegotiate the landlord's mortgage, and then offer a favourable loan to help pay for improvement, the authority had got nothing attractive to offer any of the parties. Lambeth could help somewhat with the first problem but for the second and third it hoped to interest building societies.

In the proposed General Improvement Areas this was particularly likely to apply. This is not to say that all the properties would be in multiple occupation, or that a high proportion would have expensive mortgages and lots of furnished tenants. Only that the existence of a significant number of such properties put a serious constraint on any borough-wide strategy of co-operation, and maybe even on compulsion. In the improvement areas the emphasis in the legislation is one of *co-operation* between local authorities and the owners of dwellings. Naturally this assumes that landlords or owner occupiers are in a financial position to co-operate or that they share the same views about the need to improve older property. Lambeth was trying to strengthen its bargaining position, as described earlier, by involving building societies and rehousing tenants but, because of the way building societies operate and because of the already high level of rents, this approach was likely to be less than a complete success.

The strongest sanction the local authority could use was compulsory purchase which firstly, the local party in power can be averse to using and which secondly, at the time of our work at least, central government was unwilling to approve despite a (Labour) government circular suggesting that compulsory purchase might be necessary in areas of housing stress.[25] Two compulsory purchase proposals were revoked

---

[25] 'There are a limited number of areas, mainly in large cities, where problems of physical decay are combined with problems of overcrowding and multi-occupation and other severe and intractable problems. It may

when the Conservatives came to power in Lambeth in 1968, although these may have been token gestures since the Conservative Group were subsequently involved in large compulsory purchase schemes. None of these were for the improvement of dwellings, however. Also central government has refused compulsory purchase orders for clearance schemes and referred them back to the local authority for general improvement. It remains to be seen if the same will apply to compulsory purchase for improvement or, even if some are approved, whether they are forthcoming on the required scale. Again conflict still exists at central and local level, between the need to help those in poorer property, and the need to protect the rights of property ownership.[26]

Apart from these problems even if compulsion had been politically feasible, Lambeth was faced with a crucial land shortage and could not therefore rehouse the families who were living in multiple occupation. There was thus a large gap between what Lambeth could compel landlords to do, plus what it could gain from co-operation, and what it would like to have seen improved. Much of the property was destined to remain in a poor state for a long time.

Of course much of the foregoing did not apply to the large landlords and the special institutions we have referred to. The two property companies who were operating in Lambeth had the resources to improve and the tenants who were willing to pay enhanced rents. The council helped the Duchy's problem about decanting from their redevelopment areas by rehousing a number of displaced tenants on a *quid pro quo* basis to enable it to improve or redevelop as quickly as possible. In addition the council took advantage of the Duchy's ownership of land in the

---

be necessary to make more use of compulsory purchase in such areas than in the general run of general improvement areas, depending on the facts of the situation as presented in connection with any orders submitted. As the problems of these areas are very various so the treatment would be far from uniform, and no such overall result might be possible as is to be expected in "normal" general improvement areas.' Ministry of Housing and Local Government Circular 65/69, paras. 37 and 38.

[26] The Director of Housing in Lambeth once remarked that he was waiting for some local authority to use section 72 of the 1969 Housing Act to enforce repairs on owner-occupied dwellings, adding that some would see this as an attack on individual liberty.

borough and exchanged an important site with it to make two more useful areas for housing, one for each agency.

As we saw the Church Commissioners also co-operated with the council when carrying out their housing association scheme in the borough. However none of these agencies were involved (except in a small and diminishing way on the part of the Commissioners and the Duchy) with the bottom end of the market where Lambeth's hard-core problem existed and where, as we have seen, the difficulties of incorporating the agencies concerned in the comprehensive approach were acute.

In conclusion, the main difficulties for Lambeth lay in the poor state of the rented property, the lack of resources or willingness to co-operate on the part of landlords and tenants, and a growing proportion of furnished accommodation with high rents and little security where the main problem became landlord/tenant relations and not lack of amenities. Despite the lower security of tenure given to tenants and the higher rents which could be charged, large landlords did not prefer to let furnished. When stability, steady incomes, and long-term company interests were the major goals, the higher rents and relative ease with which tenants could be removed did not compensate for the trouble that such tenancies generated. Instead the large landlord let unfurnished but used tight eligibility criteria. Furnished lettings were more the prerogative of the owner occupier wanting to let a spare room or going away for a while in Sutton, and in Lambeth of the smaller landlord intent on a quick profit, or the mortgagor who depended on a high-rental income to meet high repayments.

What we found then was a privately-rented sector where increasingly, the large landlord was gaining at one end while the poorer tenant and landlord were losing at the other. The landlords and their tenants of multi-occupied furnished properties did not have the protection of any organization behind them. Large landlords had the 'fair rent' system increasingly in their favour, tenants of large landlords had middle-class tenants' associations with professional and financial resources. The smaller landlords were rejected by estate agents because the agents had to incur unrecoverable expenses when the local authority took action. Estate agents did not regard the 'fair rent' system in the same way as larger landlords anyway. They were often more likely to switch to other activities in the face of pressure or the easy availability of alternatives and this resulted in the management of rented property playing a diminishing role in their businesses. Likewise the tenants of these smaller landlords were reluctant to co-operate with the local authority and they found that the friction which occurred in the furnished multi-occupied properties involved them in recourse to the Rent Tribunal to try and gain some security of tenure: this was increasingly the only organization which could help anybody at this bottom end of the privately-rented market. Even then the security that the Tribunal will give is strictly limited.[27]

The outlook for a comprehensive initiative in the privately-rented sector, by co-operating with or coercing private enterprise, must therefore remain rather bleak. None of our three main types of agency could or would co-operate with a borough like Lambeth in solving the *worst* problems because the agencies themselves were trying to or had managed to avoid the bottom end of the market where these problems were concentrated. Some estate agents still operated there and the qualified ones concerned were doing a useful job in transmitting the local council's demands. But it is doubtful whether these agents could

---

[27] In the study of applications to the Rent Tribunals carried out for the Francis Committee, more tenants wanted to secure their tenancy than wanted a lower rent. The Tribunals did not as a rule give the maximum permissible security—six months.

Case dismissed—no security granted	7
Up to 2 months	22
2–4 months	21
Over 4 months, under 6 months	10
6 months exactly	32
6–9 months	4
9–12 months	4

In twelve of the cases the original applications had been followed by an application for an extension of the period of security, which accounts for periods of security being over six months. No one applied for a further extension. There were also a few cases where there had been a landlord's successful application for reduction of security.

The Rent Tribunal Study formed Appendix III of the Francis Committee Report. It is also published as Adams, B., Griffin, J., and Proudman, S. *A Study of Rent Tribunal Cases in London*. Working Paper No. 68 (London: Centre for Environmental Studies, 1971). The above figures come from page 30 of that Paper.

actually achieve anything—and they were under pressure anyway to diversify in order to remain profitable.

The local authority was left to deal with the multi-occupied, often heavily mortgaged, parts of the privately-rented sector. Here the constraints on co-operation and even on being coerced were so severe and the pressures of demand for the accommodation so great, that it was virtually powerless to solve the main problems within its own boundaries, no matter how it tried to co-operate with or coerce the agencies concerned into a comprehensive approach.

References

1. FRANCIS COMMITTEE. *Report of the Committee on the Rent Acts.* Cmnd 4609 (London: H.M.S.O., 1971).

2. ZANDER, M. 'The Unused Rent Acts', *New Society*, 12 September, 1968.

3. DONNISON, D. V. 'How to Help the Poorest Tenants', *New Society*, 16 January, 1969.

4. FRANCIS COMMITTEE, op. cit., p. 43.

5. REX, J. and MOORE, R. *Race, Community, and Conflict* (Oxford: O.U.P., 1969).

Chapter Six

Private Developers

Background

Private developers have been operating in an environment closer to a free market situation than any of the other institutions we have looked at. Like the property companies and estate agents they are governed by the profit motive but, unlike the other agencies, private developers have been more or less ignored by central government. Or at most they have been encouraged to get on with the job they were doing which was assumed to be conforming to central government intentions.

In Greater London, private development has played a much smaller role than local authority development (Table 6.1). Only more recently has action been taken by central government to encourage developers to build more in the London

Table 6.1

*Local Authority and Private Sector Development. Greater London 1961–71.
Numbers of Dwellings Completed*

	Local Authorities	Private Sector
1961	22 849	10 563
1967	33 626	10 859
1968	28 003	7688
1969	22 502	6992
1970	20 677	8897
1971	21 678	9337

Source: Housing Statistics, H.M.S.O., February 1972.

area. In September 1971, the Minister of Housing and Construction said that he was prepared to see local authorities sell off land at 'less than market value', provided that developers built houses within a certain price range. He stated that:

'Over the past two years the proportion of new houses in London
built for sale has fallen from about one-third to a quarter—about
half the national average. We must surely try to give Londoners
the same opportunities for owner-occupation as the rest of the
country enjoys.' [1]

In April 1972 Mr Peter Walker announced that he was making
£80m available for local authorities to spend on assembling
land which could be released for early private development.[1]

In October 1972 a Green Paper was published on possible
methods of co-operation between councils and private companies to speed land purchase and housing development
particularly in the South-East [2]. What then can we learn
from the aims of developers and the constraints they face, of the
possibilities for more private residential development in
Greater London itself?

Aims and Operations

As we showed in the chapter on private landlords, the way
organizations satisfy the need to make profits can be operationalized in a wide variety of ways. The case is similar for
private developers. For instance, as Craven has argued [3] a
developer's attitude to growth is as significant an indication of
what, how, and where he will build as are the various constraints facing him.

The private residential housing market can be subdivided
into different price ranges. Firstly, there is the range for the
marginal buyer, £5000–£7000, probably nearer £6000–£7000
in London in 1971. Secondly, the range for existing owner
occupiers and some new owner occupiers, around £8000–
£14 000. Finally the top price bracket of £15 000 plus. However the ranking of size of developer against price range of
product is an inverse one if anything, the smaller builder
selling houses at the top to middle prices, the medium builder

---

[1] *Hansard*, Thursday, 27 April, 1972. He also announced he would be
prepared to approve compulsory purchase orders (CPOs) for land
assembly in suitable conditions especially where one landowner was
preventing suitable development by holding out or where the land was in
multiple ownership and in need of comprehensive redevelopment.

at middle to low prices, and the larger builder at the lowest prices.[2]

The part of the market the developer operates in depends to a great extent on what he is trying to achieve. On the whole the small developers we interviewed were private businesses with few if any staff beyond the owners and some secretarial assistance and they tended, increasingly, to subcontract the actual building work. The amount of money they needed to make to stay in business was relatively small and they wanted to obtain this in the easiest possible way. So the preferred strategy was to build a small number of houses in that price range which offered the highest return on capital. The best margins were not obtained in the main market where the operations of larger, more highly organized concerns with greater marketing and other resources made competition more severe but at the top end of the market. Of course the demand for this expensive housing was comparatively low and so, if these small builders had wanted to expand their organization, output, and profits they would have had to move down the market to where the mass demand existed. This might also have meant building further afield and moving out of the locality and situation they knew well, with all the attendant risks. But in the event they did not have to face this problem as they were able to make quite a good living within the restricted upper end of the market.

In contrast the large public companies we spoke to were concerned not only to maximize profits but to see them grow substantially. They had far more elaborate organizations, sometimes subdivided into different branches, including land acquisition, house construction, marketing, etc. This enabled them to handle the building of a far larger number of houses than the small men, cater for the main market, and operate over a wider geographical area—all this being essential if profits and growth were to be achieved. They were also able to carry out a more diverse range of activities to the same end in comparison with small developers. In particular we noted that companies in this bracket made some money simply from

---

[2] See the Appendix for our definition of 'small', 'medium', and 'large' developers.

buying and reselling land and one was becoming involved in the house conversion business.

The medium-sized developers were, not surprisingly, in an intermediate position. While on the one hand they preferred to build for the upper end of the market the demand here was not sufficient to fully occupy them. On the other hand the competition from the larger builders at the lower end of the market made that a difficult area to operate in so on the whole they built in the medium price range.

The details of the operations of the developers illuminates these points. Our two small builders started between eight and twelve houses per annum. This was all they both did, although one also ran a finance company which was used to support operations. The organization and staff was minute, one being a father and son partnership, the other a man and his wife. One subcontracted out all its work, the other used to have its own labour force of a handful of men but more recently subcontracted out to these men who had since set up on their own.

One of the builders felt that he could produce about twenty dwellings a year if he tried but to do this he would have to form a limited company and distribute shares and dividends which he felt would be to his own financial disadvantage. Consequently he saved the effort and spent a few months of the year abroad. He built mainly better quality flats in Sutton and other southern boroughs for between £7000 and £10 000 (£8500 for a two bedroomed one).

The other small builder built houses for between £15 000 and £20 000, plus some flats. He concentrated his activities in Sutton, he had decided that there was just as much profit in relation to hard work by building highly priced houses as by building thirty to forty cheaper houses. Each house was a one-off job, fetching in enough to keep a lucrative business going.

So far as marketing was concerned one of these builders sold the houses himself and the other relied on agents but neither had a great deal of difficulty in selling their product, since many of their customers were cash buyers or already had a home to sell. They both responded to the rocketing of prices in 1971 by setting the price for a house after completion. Neither kept a waiting list, partly because they had no real need to but partly, in one case, because he did not want customers interfering with specifications or expecting a certain price. Being as free as possible enabled him to allow for all cost increases after the dwelling was completed, with the minimum of objections.

The medium-sized builders had one or two characteristics in common with the small ones. House prices for one ranged from £10 000 and up to £15 000 in some places, although a maisonnette in Sutton could be had for £6750–£7500. Similarly the other medium firm built flats for £6750 plus, and houses for £7000–£9000. Both were thus definitely in the medium price range, one extending to the high priced although on average its prices were nearer the lower price range.

As with one of the smaller companies they sold through estate agents but one also had their own sales staff. Again most purchasers did not need mortgages or could arrange them for themselves. One company set the price for houses when they were half built. The other had been caught out by setting the price far too soon.

The three large builders were public companies and operated nationally. They built in large units, sites capable of taking less than twenty houses were excluded and all built for the bottom end of the market but showed a diversity of activities that the other developers lacked.

The smallest of the three (1000 per annum) built in the £5000–£15 000 range, mainly £5000–£12 000. They would have preferred to concentrate on more expensive houses but the size of the market precluded this. Rather than expanding profits via an expansion of housebuilding they had turned to land speculation and had a whole section devoted to this activity. They also had commercial and industrial development companies, as well as doing contracting work for local authorities. They sold most of their own houses and had a quota of mortgages given them by one large building society (about £500 000 per annum). This was very useful in a mortgage famine but we were told that this was equally in the interests of the building society. In the somewhat rare circumstances when they have more money to lend than normal they hope that the large developers will take more from them.

The largest company, building 12 000 per annum had to cater for the mass market in order to expand output and profits. They had their own sales organization and also got quotas from the five largest building societies to facilitate this.

They had also diversified into council contracting and expanded internationally.

The third company (3000 per annum) had diversified in every way possible. It built all over the country. In London it built flats in the £6000–£10 000 range, houses in the £10 000–£14 000 plus range. It was making flats out of one or two houses in Inner London. It was involved in some redevelopment in Outer London (thirty unit minimum sites) and 60 per cent of its dwelling output in London was flats. It was part of a group whose market value in 1963 was £1.6m but which was worth £130m by 1971. The man behind it all had built his empire by selling off properties in 1963 which might be affected by a Labour Government introducing rent restrictions and buying national and international industrial and development companies, particularly when the company concerned had management problems. While the profit margin was far easier to obtain at the top end of the residential market, this company for growth reasons concentrated on the mass market. It also had a building society quota and did its own marketing.

There were also large firms which did not necessarily want to grow any bigger and these could settle down to more of a middle range of house prices, as well as including some mass market products to help the turnover. One we knew of built 1000 per annum, from £4000–£14 000, but their buyers were more typically second time purchasers in the middle to top executive range, less affected by increases in national unemployment rates, or local redundancies than the mass market. Another firm built between 800 to 1000 houses per annum but used the same criteria as the previous one. In fact in 1972 it completed a block of fifty-six flats in St John's Wood (N.W. London), and the cheapest of these was over £14 000. By this time though the firm had stopped growing and had been keen to project an image of greater 'social responsibility'. It had, for example, been one of the first private enterprise firms to start backing housing associations.

The motivation or lack of motivation for growth and the problems and methods of achieving it can only be comprehended in the light of an understanding of the constraints private developers face. It is to this that we now turn.

Problems and Constraints

There are four main and interconnected factors which together, with differing degrees of importance, determine the rather distinctive patterns of operation of the developers. They are, the financial basis of the company, the person or body to whom they are accountable, the organization of the company and, finally, the availability of the particular type of land that the company requires for its operations. In addition the institution of nationally agreed minimum standards for house building has, as we shall see, created problems for some builders.

The small privately-owned developers had no problem in securing money, obtaining it from their own capital, in one case from their own finance company or, when hard pressed, from the clearing banks. As the returns that they were making were satisfactory there was no pressure to expand—as they were only accountable regarding the profits they made to themselves. Indeed the financial risks they might then have to take were a positive disincentive to expansion. Once a small company starts expanding there is often a problem of finance and of high interest rates which can lead to great difficulties in a time of credit famine.

The large builders were all large-scale public companies requiring a great deal of working capital. So far as financing was concerned they—like the small builders—seemed to have few problems, though we must remember that at the time of our research the industry was on an upswing. They could rely on internal financing or on a bank overdraft—in some cases, where the firm was part of a large group, interest was paid to the holding company at bank rate plus a small margin. However their public status meant that, unlike the small men, they were accountable to shareholders and, in general, to the state of stock-market opinion regarding their prospects. This was one of the main incentives behind the desire and need of these firms to expand, for expansion attracts investment. In fact the diversity of their operations was a response to this need. For example the largest company needed to turn over its capital one and a half times a year to produce the dividends they required and this partially explains why they catered for the mass market, only built on large sites which were less trouble to develop, and minimized their involvement in time-consuming schemes such as the building of flats.[3]

The smallest of the three larger companies as we saw had turned to land speculation, seeing that good profits were to be made in the conditions of shortage and high prices in the South-East. The third of the larger companies, being a part of a fast-growing group, was expected by both the group head and the stock market to make fast and growing profits. This was why the company as we saw, was forced to diversify to the utmost. The financial constraints of a development company are determined by the head of the company who will attract investment according to his aims. The acquisitive leadership attracts the kind of investment which requires quick profits. Assets have to be diversified to keep the profits coming and in house building the mass market provided the quickest returns.

In many ways the medium-sized companies were in the most difficult situation. By being public companies they shared the same need as the larger companies to grow but their financial basis was not as secure as the larger companies. As a result they had a more difficult time, being less able to take risks in land speculation for instance. This can be seen from the example of one of these companies who would have been quite happy to see its civil engineering side outgrow all its other activities. However it had to keep the private residential company ticking over because all parts of a quoted group of companies had to be self-supporting, a fall in one would affect the security of the others. For this reason no one company within the group financed another. Internal financing was the norm but from within each company. The residential company was finding most schemes 'difficult' anyway, so borrowing from outside sources was a non-starter since interest had to be paid at $1\frac{1}{3}$ per cent per month while any problems were sorted out. For the same reason they did not speculate in land, since this was viewed as gambling, and the penalty if it did not pay off was high interest payments and no price appreciation.

Organizational problems also affected the operations of

---

[3] These might take up to fifteen months to develop (for a block of forty), with no one in occupation until all were complete, whereas on a new estate the first house was up and occupied within twenty weeks.

some of the companies. The small local builders with minimal staff, operating in and around the local area had few difficulties but the medium-sized firms, which were originally locally based, were being forced to go further afield in the search for profits because of their public status and the need for growth. They found that problems of effective site supervision grew as they did. So they began to require the more elaborate organization and expertise that the larger companies had without necessarily having the resources to achieve this. Obviously the move from private to public status imposes a whole new set of constraints on a company which it may find difficult to negotiate.

The large companies had far more elaborate organizations and here a different problem tended to arise. In particular there was a great pressure on them to keep their labour force and plant fully occupied. In times of difficulty the small private firms could contract their operations fairly easily, employing few if any full-time staff. This option is less available to a large and complex company which requires a certain level of stability if its organization is not to be broken up. The increasing concentration on land speculation and the concurrent decision to stabilize rather than continue to expand housebuilding by one company was partially a reaction to this problem, as was their diversification into other building and engineering work. The largest company, while also diversifying, had become something of a 'building machine', finding itself with an urgent need to acquire land at a rapid rate in order to keep its considerable organization fully employed.[4]

Of course the actions of central government also affected the financial situation of the companies. The course of economic policy affects the prospects of the construction industry especially in the residential sector via the amount of money the building societies have available and therefore the extent to which there is an effective demand for new housing. Also the interest companies have to pay on the money they borrow is an important factor. All these problems are likely to be easier for

---

4 One of the other large firms had recently sold this firm a sixty-acre golf-course in Leeds for £675 000. The large firm did not even phase the payment and acquisition period because of the demand for land for more or less immediate use.

larger companies to cope with as they have resources to do so, or possibly for the small men who can easily cut back on their commitments and who are likely to be selling at the top end of the market anyway, where profit margins are higher and the demand for mortgage finance lower.

Apart from these constraints, however, there is one other government backed feature of the private developer's working environment which has created a significant problem for some of them. In 1966 the Minister of Housing and Local Government announced that the Building Societies Association had agreed to recommend to its members that mortgages should be made available only to people buying homes built by developers who were registered with the National House Builders Registration Council. A subsequent threat by the government that compulsion would be applied if builders did not join the NHBRC voluntarily meant that most builders have now become members.[5]

The membership by 1971 had reached 15 000. Since 1967 between thirty and forty builders had been expelled and admission refused to 400. Since expulsion virtually means bankruptcy, larger builders overcame their problems. Most expulsions are among the small builders but several are medium-sized builders. In fact since, according to the NHBRC, there are only seventy builders in the country who build over 250 houses per annum, the medium-sized builder was over-represented in expulsions. Small builders do proportionately rather well since, although they form most of those expelled, they number thousands as members of NHBRC. Other small builders of course, who build for the market which is not dependent on mortgage money have little reason to join any-

---

[5] The Council has a ten-year guarantee scheme. By 1970 over two million people lived in houses carrying the ten-year guarantee. The service included precautionary spot-check inspections of houses, the provision of minimum standards for a house (more socket outlets, more space in kitchens, external treatment of joinery), a two-year warranty of £5000 per house for major or minor defects which an independent arbitrator judged to be due to non-compliance with the Council's requirements, and a further warranty from the third to the tenth year of up to £2500 per house against the cost of making good any damage caused by a major structural defect.

way. Their houses are probably of a high standard in any case, particularly the most expensive ones.

However, the NHBRC has been prevented from pushing its standards up too high because it is estimated that the adoption of full Parker Morris standards would put over £400 on the price of the basic house. In this it has probably had the interests of the consumer at heart, but the decision has most likely saved many more, particularly medium-sized builders, from expulsion. The more competition is made difficult for firms trying to grow or maintain a certain slice of the market, the more the extra cost has to come out of profit margins. The firms either cannot benefit from the economies of scale of the larger firms or they lack the resources to make good any large defects.

The most important set of constraints for all builders are those connected with the supply of land. This divides into a number of different aspects including obtaining information about available land, assessing the right price to pay for the land, and finding the right type of land for the market the company is building for in the right size and condition for its scale of operations. It was the outcome of the builders' attempts to solve these problems which, in the context of the other problems we have discussed, tended to have the greatest effect on what they would build and therefore on the then current and future role of private residential development in Greater London as a whole and in our two boroughs in particular.

The first point is that in the South-East generally there is a shortage of suitable land for development. However this definition of suitable land will vary from one developer to another. Thus the small builders only require, indeed only have the resources to acquire, small sites. Infilling in existing low-density housing areas is the ideal strategy for them. Because of the market they build for these must be in 'quality' residential areas and the sites must be well serviced as they are rarely willing to contribute to new roads or other public services. Here it is important to realize that the price any builder pays for land is a residual cost, i.e. he decides how much he can sell the houses he wants to build for, deducts building, marketing, and other costs from this, adds his profit margin, and what he is left with is the amount he will pay for the land. In the sort of area in which the small builder can operate, land costs will be high already and so the need to pay for additional services may well make the whole deal uneconomic.

Given the shortage of land an effective intelligence system is at a premium. The small builders we spoke to had the advantage over the larger companies of a detailed knowledge of the local area in which they operated and also had good contacts with local estate agents who, apart from getting a commission on the land they found, often benefited by handling the ensuing sales.

In Outer London generally, much of the available land is in the form of small infill sites and the 'quality' of this area is generally regarded as high. Obviously then this will be the best environment for the small builder to operate in, although because of the overall shortage even our small Sutton builders found they were having to move further and further afield in their search for suitable sites.

The medium-sized builders were also being increasingly forced to move further away from London and even the Home Counties in their search for land. They were getting to the size where it was becoming very expensive to build one-off houses on small sites because of labour diseconomies of small scale. So when they did get small sites the medium-sized builders tended to build blocks of flats on them. They also used agents as their main source of information and the further away they moved from their London base the more this was necessary. As with the small builders they were mainly looking for land which was 'ripe' for development, land which did not require much in the way of new services, and which either already had planning permission or where permission could be easily obtained. For, unlike the large firms neither the small or medium builders could afford to take risks on land which the local authority might not agree to them developing, nor could they hold a large stock of land for several years until the market conditions were right for building.

The large companies catering for the mass market would have found it uneconomic to develop small infill sites. Their organization was not adapted to producing one-off or small-group housing. In addition they were catering for the mass market and the cost of small infill sites was prohibitive for this type of market. So they were mainly looking for virgin sites with a minimum size of about ten acres. Such sites were rare even in outer boroughs such as Sutton and so these companies built very little in London at all.

Given the intense competition between the large developers for land and the relatively small profit margins in the mass market in which they operated, an efficient system for finding suitable sites and assessing their market potential was required. They used estate agents and also went out and looked for land but they seemed to have developed different degrees of sophistication in their understanding and methods of approaching the problem.

All the firms started by trying to forecast what the demand for houses was, or was likely to be in a particular area. This was then measured against the price of house the company had to sell in order to achieve its aims. The largest developer we spoke to, for instance, carried out sophisticated market research. It avoided single-industry towns and calculated the average industrial wage in an area. If this was less than the building society monthly repayments on houses of the type it could profitably build, it built elsewhere. We were told about one firm which used census data and other statistics to identify 'dynamic areas'. Migration patterns were analysed, commuting patterns discovered, and estimates of future patterns were made in the light of possible development in the area. Then the target market's capacity to pay was assessed, and designed to, provided of course it was in the interests of the firm to build for this particular price range.

Unlike the small and medium firms the large firms were not only interested in buying land which was 'ripe' for immediate development. They also all had land 'banks' consisting of sites in various degrees of readiness or suitability for development. There were three main reasons for having a stock of land. Firstly, it ensured a continuing supply of land for their future operations. This was the main motive for the largest 'building machine' type company which had £20–£30m tied up in its bank. Secondly, it enabled profits to be made simply from buying and selling the stock of land. The firm which had diversified into this activity illustrates this most clearly. They were buying and assembling larger sites for the other developers to whom they would later sell. They felt that they could buy any land in the South-East because the shortage was so acute. Any site disadvantages would be offset by sheer demand. They would not buy individual houses but larger areas of non-'ripe' land, which they would hold for several years, during which time they would consult with the local authority or with other developers about the eventual comprehensive plans for the area.

Finally, it was not possible for these developers to find enough already 'ripe' land for their operations. This meant that they had to buy ahead of immediate needs and wait for, and take an active part in, the 'ripening' process. Essentially there are two elements in this process. The first is obtaining planning permission; this is where the big developer can play an active role in persuading the local authority to agree to grant permission, if necessary appealing to the Ministry on refusal and even resubmitting applications time and time again until the council agree. While this is a risky business it can clearly be profitable, for the value of the land, either for resale or for the firm's own use, is far greater when this permission is obtained. The second and less controllable factor involves waiting for the demand for housing to increase to a stage where it is economic to build on normally 'inferior' land. Although developers have land they will not use it until it makes 'financial sense' to do so. Land bought up in various old portfolios might not be in what developers consider to be the right place. Even land close to profitable areas can be made useless so far as developers are concerned, because demand varies according to very localized factors. One developer demonstrated how detailed some of these calculations had to be. He said that towns expanded radially until they reached a major boundary, going from shopping centres to motorway intersections or railway lines. Boundaries varied in their ability to supercede other boundaries. A motorway built the other side of a railway for instance, would mean that development will leapfrog the railway line and move up to the motorway, but not the other way round. Land prices and development potential would therefore vary within very short distances. In other words, the demand for any houses on a site would vary according to the relationship of the site to major boundaries. Similarly a change in the catchment area of a school was considered to alter the 'micro-market' limitations. In the South-East more unattractive land was being used simply because everything completely desirable (no barriers impeding development or factors affecting value) had been used up. But developers nevertheless hung on to what they had until demand had risen sufficiently to compensate for its undesirable location.[6]

Skill, resources, and time are all required to negotiate these problems and only the larger developers had all three. But to a large extent it is only the larger, growth oriented concerns catering for the mass market, with a public status and shareholders to satisfy, who have to face up to the full complexities of the land market.

The territorial implications of these constraints, especially those concerning land acquisition, are clear now. Some builders using infill sites and specializing in small groups of flats or expensive houses had the right aims, size of organization, and could afford to pay the higher prices required for land in London. They were gradually moving further and further out as infill sites were exhausted but this is a slow process. On the other hand medium and large builders committed to expansion had to cater for the mass market where the largest demand for new housing existed. This market demanded the cheapest possible housing and since land is a residual cost, the developers had to find cheap land[7] and large sites to cut overheads, and there were few of these left in the metropolitan area.

The Limitations of a Comprehensive Housing Policy

We were not able to collect data from our developers about whom they housed but some indirect references have already been made to this in the preceding sections and some points will be taken up again in this section.

In most other chapters we have concentrated the discussion

---

[6] It is the operation of this factor which explains a part of the apparent discrepancy between local authorities' claims that they have released sufficient land for development in the South-East and developers' claims that there is a persistent shortage.

[7] The economic point is a simple one. The mass market consists of very many first-time purchasers who cannot afford to compete with wealthier people who want to live close to the centre. Since wealthier people can pay more for housing, the price the developers who are building the more expensive houses can pay for land is correspondingly higher. The result is a two-way process with the needs of the supplier and the purchaser coming together to determine a certain pattern of residential development.

on agencies operating within Lambeth and Sutton. In this chapter we have had to take a wider view because what we have to explain is the lack of private-sector development in Lambeth and the very limited opportunities that appeared to be available (mainly for small local builders) in Sutton. We needed to see where, under what conditions, and by whom private housing was being built in order to produce this explanation. We have seen that in general opportunities for large-scale profit making by private developers in London were poor and it should therefore come as no surprise to find that these housing agencies, which are purely market oriented and which more than any other have neither assumed any 'social' role nor had one enforced on them by government, were doing very little in London. On the other hand small local builders could still exist. In Inner London, where even infill sites were rare, many of them were producing new and converted flats and in Outer London flats and expensive houses were more common.[8] Furthermore these units were very expensive and are only available for upper socio-economic groups.[9] So the contribution of new private development to the mass demand from young family buyers with moderate incomes in London was likely to be a small one and the prospects for any comprehensive housing policy in London which was based on an alternative expectation of the situation in Lambeth and Sutton was poor. The policies of Lambeth and Sutton councils towards private development illustrates and amplifies this conclusion.

As we have seen 500 of Lambeth's target of 2000 new dwellings per year were planned to come from the private sector, including houses built for sale by private developers.[10] However the main concentration of new private housing in

---

[8] Our building society data showed that in Inner London 16 per cent of all secondhand housing is in the form of flats but 60 per cent of all new housing is of this type. In Outer London the figures are 10 per cent and 46 per cent respectively.

[9] According to our building society data the average price of the new housing in the Greater London area which received society mortgages in 1970 was £7169. This is likely to underestimate the average of all new building as many of the higher-priced dwellings will have been bought outright or by arrangements with insurance companies.

[10] This is because, according to the Chairman of the Housing Committee, 24 per cent of people in clearance areas were owner occupiers.

Inner London was in boroughs like Camden, Kensington and Chelsea, Westminster, and Lewisham, areas with an attractive environment and substantial concentrations of middle-class housing. Lambeth had relatively few existing areas with the attractions of the other boroughs and, except in the South, few areas of middle-class housing. In fact Lambeth found that developers were only willing to pay £35 000 per acre for land, whereas the cost to the council would be £60 000 (and clearance would double it); they would only build to very low densities, only on the most attractive sites not adjacent to council property, and they would not restrict their sales to residents of Lambeth. We can now see how Lambeth's experience fits into the general situation that developers faced.

Lambeth had the choice of approaching small, medium, or large-scale developers. With all the developers the price calculations left too large a gap between what a developer can pay for land after deducting his costs from the price of a house, and what the land would cost the council to get ready for building. Even with a subsidy on the cost of the land, it is doubtful whether firstly, builders would be encouraged to build on otherwise unattractive sites (it is expected that most clearance areas in boroughs like Lambeth will be in 'risky' areas) or secondly, whether the cost will be reduced to the level that developers can look twice at. The slum clearance subsidy in the 1972 Housing Finance Act might well bear out the first point. Under the Act local authorities are allowed to dispose of the land as they wish, instead of having to build council houses on it. But it is a *slum* clearance subsidy. Unless the authority then invests a considerable amount of money in improving the surrounding area (and this eliminates land badly needed for other, maybe public housing or for industrial use), no developer would be interested. The subsidy is 75 per cent of the cost of clearance and, while this may just cover the cost in some areas, in others there will still be an excess which developers could not cover. Clearance of obsolete or multi-occupied dwellings for general planning use under the existing planning law only qualifies for a 50 per cent subsidy and since, as we saw in Chapter One, *slum* clearance was playing an increasingly smaller part in redevelopment in many boroughs like Lambeth their potential for encouraging private developers was restricted even further.

But there are additional reasons why developers would not

be interested even if these problems were overcome. Given the goals of small developers we discussed earlier, there is no point in trying to interest them in expanding. Secondly, they are happier in no-risk areas—there is no logical reason why they should move their activities since there is plenty of demand in Outer London. Private houses built for sale in Lambeth have never exceeded 250 (the figure reached in 1966) and by 1971 the figure had dropped to 150. If more of them did move they would go into the better boroughs already mentioned. Anyway, as we have seen, they built expensive, luxury houses and the relatively more expensive flats—not the kind that people from redevelopment areas or from council houses can afford. Increasing permissible densities would not solve the problems, for this merely affects what the developer can pay for land, not what price he will ask for a house. It means that he can afford more for the land. In fact part of the explanation for the recent rise in land prices for the London 0–20 mile zone, is the increase in median density from eleven dwellings per acre in 1965–66 to fourteen dwellings per acre in 1971. The density rating for the 21–40 mile zone was about the same for the three sets of years contained in the table.[11]

Medium-sized builders need to move to areas where there is more land. The ones we studied found it hard in Sutton, so they would find it even more difficult in Lambeth. In order to expand they have to move outwards rather than inwards, or develop another type of product. If they do this then they must retain their slice of the market to keep the whole group of companies an attractive investment proposition. High costs, risky areas, and no land, mean that the medium group—the most vulnerable of all the developers because they are in a transitional stage—would not be interested in Inner London.

[11] *Median Prices per Plot (£)*

	1965–66	1966–67	1970
London (0–20 miles)	1825	2400	5416
London (21–40 miles)	1525	2400	4178
Birmingham (0–12 miles)	1637	1520	2216
Birmingham (13–25 miles)	1170	1200	2022

Source: *The Estates Gazette*, 15 April, 1972, pp. 94 and 95.

Our large-scale developers needed a certain plot size to justify development. Even if this could be provided in Lambeth, and this is not very probable, the most likely development in Inner London, as is happening in Outer London, is the construction of flats. That is the only way for a larger builder to get the densities as high as he can to justify the investment. The largest developer we discussed could not build flats because of the time they took to fill with residents. The other large builders we knew of built them at far too high a price. This is to be expected when a site is large enough and sufficiently attractive to justify investment by a large developer as he will cater for the largest chunk of demand in the attractive areas and that in London in 1970/71 put prices of family-sized flats at £14 000 at their lowest.

The basic problem was that Lambeth lacked the ability to bargain with developers. The LCC managed to get developers to give them expensive sites for residential development in exchange for planning permission for office blocks in the days before the office boom was curtailed in 1965. But Lambeth had nothing the developers wanted.

One way which offered some hope for Lambeth to increase the proportion of new housing for sale was for the council to build the houses for sale itself. The first phase of an experimental scheme of fifty houses were being built for sale at £8000–£9000 but the new Labour local administration stopped the scheme in 1971 after seventeen had been completed. However even at these prices it must be doubted whether there would be sufficient local demand for an expansion of the programme. This is borne out by the fact that although all the eventual purchasers were Lambeth residents 75 per cent of the applicants did not live in the borough and in fact there were only just enough Lambeth residents to fill the scheme. So further development would be likely to involve the importation of population. This might satisfy the planner's goal of 'social mix' but would conflict with the other policy of population reduction.

The main problem for a local authority in London trying to provide houses for owner occupation to people in council houses, or to first-time purchasers, is to get the price low enough. The obvious developer to approach is either the medium or large scale one. Sutton in fact embarked on a scheme to sell the land for private house development at 'less than market value'. Properties were to be sold on 99-year leases, with financial help coming from low ground rents [4]. Densities were to be between fifty and seventy persons per acre to encourage the larger developer and to obtain the most dwellings. One hundred per cent mortgages were to be made available. The land was to be built on within a certain period of time and not used as a land bank. The scheme was to be restricted to existing council tenants, people on the housing waiting list, and young couples.

The problems involved here are twofold. Firstly, the house could be turned into a quick capital gain by the purchaser and resold. This means that Sutton's aim of extending home owner-ship could have had a very limited future—one family's occupation. Consequently there had to be safeguards against this, and this brought in the second problem. The authority could impose a long-term covenant to ensure its right of purchase at below market price, or it could say that the initial buyer should sell on the market but repay the original subsidy. Sutton had powers under a private Act of 1951 to require covenants which could bind first and subsequent buyers. Any such covenant must extend beyond the five years normal in the sale of council houses to tenants and in this case they would have lasted for twenty-one years.[12]

Another difficulty the policy found was that the builders would no longer assess the open market price and demand for their product. An estimate would be made on 'controlled' assumptions—that certain people in council houses or waiting lists would be willing and able to buy. This might well have been the case, especially with rapid rent increases, but the extent was unknown and made the enterprise unpredictable.

---

[12] If owners wish to sell in the first eight years, the houses bought at 30 per cent discount will have to be offered back to the council at the original price with adjustments up or down for deterioration. For the remaining thirteen years the home still has to be offered to the council at the prevailing market price less the original discount and a proportion of the increase in value—e.g. a family who buys a four-bedroomed house for £11 200 and sells to the council after nine years at £25 000 would receive £17 000, forfeiting the original 30 per cent discount of £4800 and 30 per cent of the £9000 appreciation—£7500 in all. *The Guardian*, 22 December, 1972.

On top of this, the greater the restrictions on resale, the greater the unpredictability for the builder.

As a result there had to be a compromise between three goals: that of the consumer, of the builder, and of the local authority. Sutton had managed to get one or two developers interested according to the Leader of the Council. It seems that Sutton's contribution to the Greater London effort hung on the encouragement of private residential development along these lines. In which case the success of the policy depended on how many restrictions the developer was prepared to accept. This was uncertain at the time of our research.

However we believe that it is unlikely that in the long term many families will benefit, since the compromise will most probably be in the developer's favour, as his is the organization which has what other people want. Only to the extent that he is really desperate for land or has no alternatives to invest in, would he concede to conditions not established by the criteria of the private market.

The GLC have few direct opportunities to intervene in this sector. In the light of the conclusions of this chapter their exhortations in the Greater London Development Plan that 'private enterprise . . . should be encouraged to assist the efforts of the public housing authorities' [5] seemed to be a call which is unlikely to meet with any significant response. More positively the GLC have recently called for legislation to allow councils to sell at up to 20 per cent below market price even if this means taking a loss and to extend the covenant on resale from five to ten years to prevent profiteering [6]. As we have argued, to the extent that this increases the constraints on the developer it adds to doubts about whether this approach can make a significant contribution to extending home ownership in London.

In successive chapters of this book we have examined the implications for comprehensive housing policies of the actions of a wide range of agencies, from those committed to some sort of ideology related to housing need (local authorities, housing associations) to those whose attitudes, though basically commercially motivated, have elements of some social concern incorporated in them (building societies) or imposed on them by government (landlords and agents), and finally to private developers. The developers represent the opposite extreme to the local authorities, being primarily concerned with profit and unfettered by any significant pressure to deviate from this concern. The case of the developers in London is the clearest example of the limitations that the need to co-operate with private enterprise put on any of the three councils' concept of a comprehensive housing policy.

References

1. *The Guardian*, 1 October, 1971.
2. Department of the Environment. *Report of Working Party on Local Authority/Private Enterprise Partnership Schemes* (London: H.M.S.O., 1972).
3. CRAVEN, E. 'Private Residential Expansion in Kent' in *Whose City?* R. Pahl (editor) (London: Longmans, 1970).
4. *The Guardian*, 10 March, 1973.
5. GLDP. *Written Statement* (London: GLC, 1969), para. 3.20, p. 17.
6. *The Guardian*, 28 October, 1972.

PART THREE

Conclusions

Chapter Seven

The Limitations
of Change

Introduction

In this study we have examined the responses of three local
authorities and a wide variety of other housing agencies to the
concept of a 'comprehensive approach' to housing policy. In
the Introduction we outlined three different interpretations of
this approach. We also linked the generation of these differing
approaches with the interaction between party politics, per-
ceptions of the type and level of housing needs which it was felt
housing policy should be dealing with, and the distribution of
political power within the local authority. In our discussion of
the housing agencies concerned we concentrated on examining
the impact that ideologies and constraints had on their operations, in the belief that an understanding of these factors was
important if the viability of the roles that housing agencies were
being asked to play was to be assessed. In this chapter we shall
examine the prospects for changes within the organization of
housing which will improve housing opportunities in the context of the complex system we have outlined. The first task is to
bring together the substantive findings of our research in order
to arrive at a general conclusion about the factors which affect
the housing opportunities which people have.

The Territorial Distribution of Housing Opportunities

An individual's socio-economic status is clearly one of the
prime determinants of his housing opportunities. Our data
showed that the level of income and correspondingly the
type of occupation required for house purchase, for example,

or admission to the 'respectable' end of the privately-rented sector, was greater than that required for public-sector housing. However this relationship between socio-economic status and housing is a generally accepted and uncontroversial point. What has our research added to the understanding of what other factors determine housing opportunities?

In Lambeth we saw how the local authority decided to concentrate on a massive effort to solve its housing problems. As a result, it developed a housing policy which contained, among its major aims, securing as much help as possible from other agencies, reducing the resident population, and expanding its own public housing programme. So far as this last aim was concerned we saw that there were significant problems which severely limited the extent to which this expansion could be achieved.

In Sutton the picture was very different. Public housing was regarded as a residual provision for those unfortunate enough to be unable to provide for themselves. The Housing Department was solely concerned with the public sector and the size of its programme was determined both by the politicians' wish to keep the rate deficit on the housing revenue account as low as possible and by the political opposition to more council estates. On the other hand owner occupation was encouraged and the council tried to help low-income buyers by a generous mortgage scheme and by subsidizing building land.

In the general metropolitan area the GLC had the duty, under the 1963 London Government Act, of overseeing the needs of London as a whole, as well as some more specific powers which it had on a transitional basis. In strategic terms its main task was clear, to help the hard pressed inner boroughs by giving them nominations to its own housing stock, much of it in Outer London, and helping with building new houses in the inner areas. We saw how the operations of the GLC provided a major source of housing for those in the inner areas but how the initiative of the original Labour administration at County Hall to persuade or cajole the outer boroughs to build and allocate more for the needs of the inner city had not been continued or extended under the Conservative council. The previous analysis of policies in Sutton provided an illustration of why this possibility had met with resistance from many Outer London boroughs.

The local authority mortgage schemes varied as much as their public housing programme but in rather different ways. Because of the influence of officers outside the Housing Directorate Lambeth's mortgage scheme signally failed to help the marginal buyer and to encourage people to move out of the borough. The GLC and Sutton schemes helped poorer buyers far more and contributed to moving people out of inner areas, although they had no explicit aim of doing so. In Sutton and the GLC the political goals of expanding owner occupation *per se* led to the generous schemes which obviously helped to attract people from all over London—especially from boroughs where the mortgage scheme was as restrictive as Lambeth's was.

Housing associations have played an increasing role in the provision of housing in London in the past few years but they still produce only a tiny proportion of the numbers required. We saw that there were few opportunities for them to carry out new building in Inner London although they did succeed in doing this in Sutton. The future contribution that the associations could make in the inner city was limited by the number of properties available for conversion. In addition at the time of our research the movement was largely unco-ordinated with a good deal of rivalry and wasteful competition between associations financed from different sources. The quality of their administration varied greatly, as did the motives of their organizers. In Lambeth the council had made a determined effort to overcome many of these difficulties and had used their power to withhold loans in order to bring the associations' work in line with the borough's overall housing strategy. However the GLC, for political reasons, were less concerned to attach strong conditions to their loans and this attitude had led to some disruption of Lambeth's policies. Unlike the above mentioned two authorities the Sutton associations—in line with local political priorities—rarely provided accommodation for general needs and the council had, with some success, encouraged them to provide for old people as this was thought to be one of the major needs in the area.

The building societies were bound by a set of rules and traditions, some of them imposed by government, but their ideological predispositions were overwhelmingly important and made them unwilling to lend widely in inner areas except on very expensive property. The situation was easier in the outer areas where the authorities had less need to ask for co-operation but even here it was difficult to get a loan on older housing and in fact an increasing number of the mortgages they granted were for non-family housing.

Private landlords varied. The larger ones were well organized and, whether operating in Inner or Outer London they had exploited the fair rent system and supporting measures to their benefit. It seemed certain that a small, high quality, privately-rented sector provided both by property companies and the older 'estates' would continue to exist in order to serve higher-income professionals, foreign visitors, and similar people. In contrast the bulk of the privately-rented sector was in decline and this particularly affected Lambeth. The very legislation that helped the larger landlords was putting impossible demands on the smaller and poorer landlords. The increasing control over their activities by local government which we saw in Lambeth, while being a justifiable attempt to improve conditions for the tenants, often became merely another pressure persuading the landlord to sell out. For the tenants in the bulk of the privately-rented sector in Lambeth, especially those in furnished property, the situation seemed to be getting worse rather than better, since the local authority had little to offer apart from encouraging people to move out of its area.

Finally private residential developers also varied greatly in the type of housing that they were providing in different areas but few of them saw much opportunity or had much inclination to build more in Inner London except at the top end of the market. The situation was also worsening in Outer London where the cost and supply of land was forcing them to leave the city altogether and even the relatively small local firms in Sutton were beginning to look elsewhere.

What emerges clearly from this summary of the attitudes and operations of the agencies is that, given an individual's socio-economic status, there will be great variation in his housing opportunities depending on the area in which he is living. The outcome of the interaction of the ideologies of the housing agencies and the constraints operating on them is a geographically differentiated distribution of opportunities.

What this means for individuals has emerged from our examination of the characteristics of those housed by agencies

in Inner and Outer London. A Londoner's housing opportunities will be greatly affected by spatial factors regardless of
whether he is in the public or private sector. The availability of
adequate local authority housing will depend, for instance,
given the qualification rules, on the borough in which he finds
himself.

For example, despite a vigorous local authority housing
programme in Lambeth the shortage of land led to a strategy
of maximizing housing gain on clearance sites. This meant a
concentration on areas where sharing was not at its most
intense and a building programme of small dwellings to cater
for the demand from the older tenants in the selected clearance
areas. So small- and medium-sized families on low and moderate incomes could hope, eventually, to be offered council
housing in Lambeth. Of course they might have to wait a long
time for this and in the meantime they were often living in
very poor conditions. The GLC and the outer boroughs also
offered the possibility of rehousing in Outer London for both
large and small families but larger poorer families were unlikely
to be able to move out. It was this group as well who could not
find public housing in Inner London and who were accordingly
dependent on the privately-rented sector, where opportunities
also varied from area to area. In the outer boroughs there was
very little furnished and not a great deal of unfurnished
accommodation generally available and in Inner London
poorer people might find themselves in unequal competition
with other, more affluent, would-be tenants.

The level and type of housing association activity also varied
from area to area, with 'specialist' associations in Sutton, for
instance, and 'general needs' ones in Lambeth. But in particular low-income tenants could not be rehoused by the
associations in Lambeth because of the financial constraints the
associations faced.

Thus the second main part of our research has also demonstrated that geographical position is vital in the determination
of housing opportunities for the individual because the ideologies held by and the constraints operating on the agencies which
make these opportunities available result in them distributing
opportunities in a geographically distinct pattern.

The Territorial Distribution of Housing Policies and Housing Needs

Housing opportunities varied from area to area but this is not the only component of the housing system which varies in this way. Of course the intensity of housing need is different in different areas as well and our research and much other work has shown this to be the case. Lambeth and other Inner London areas contain problems which are far more severe than anything to be found in Sutton or the other outer boroughs.

However it is the territorial distribution of housing policies and in particular the specific approach adopted by local authorities to the concept of comprehensive policies which forms the final link in the series of factors which we are analysing. All the three authorities whose policies we discuss, the GLC, Lambeth, and Sutton, were Conservative controlled for at least half the period covered by our research. If housing policy was merely a reflection of political outlook we would expect to see great similarities between the three authorities' approaches to their housing responsibilities. This was not the case for as we saw Lambeth had a 'regulatory' approach whereas the GLC and Sutton both sought to promote different brands of a 'co-operative' approach. In each case the political outlook was affected by the different levels of housing need in the three areas within which each local authority was operating and this factor was capable in Lambeth's case of greatly modifying the sort of housing policies that a Conservative administration might naturally be expected to follow.

Lambeth's Conservatives faced a situation where there were pressing needs which had to be met by local authority action of some sort and this was impressed upon them by an 'activist' Housing Director who was allowed access to key politicians. Of course, the Sutton Conservatives' policies were also determined by housing needs but these were wholly different in the outer borough. Most people could find satisfactory solutions to their housing needs in the private sector. This being so the need for local authority intervention was less evident. In fact there was a minimal level of public housing provision which probably underestimated the level of need that actually existed. On the other hand anything the local authority could do to improve access to private-sector housing had obvious political appeal and as we saw Sutton council's comprehensive concept was almost wholly of this nature. It was thought that the need that existed could be ameliorated by relying on the private sector. Chief officers who might have thought differently were not given the same degree of influence on policy making as in Lambeth. The Housing Manager for most of the time remained a 'second tier' chief officer.

The GLC wanted to follow a similar 'co-operative' approach to that of Sutton. As we saw it encouraged housing associations and made its mortgage scheme very generous, while tending to be far less energetic than its Labour predecessor in public housing matters. But the GLC policy, while avoiding the degree of intervention that Lambeth practised, had at least to appear to show more concern than Sutton did for the problems of those who could not find private-sector solutions. The fact that the GLC had responsibility for some aspects of housing in both Inner and Outer London meant that, although a Conservative GLC would naturally tend to identify with outer areas and with the policies and outlook of councils in these areas (such as Sutton), they could not entirely ignore the political consequences that would follow if they did. In the event the GLC seemed in practical terms to place emphasis on versions of a 'co-operative' policy which did not bring them into too much conflict with the outer boroughs, while maintaining enough activity for the benefit of inner areas to be able to claim that they were not ignoring their statutory duties towards these areas.

Policies, Needs, and Opportunities

Therefore what has emerged from our research is a system of housing in London which can be seen to be composed of three elements, all of which have a distinct territorial distribution. Firstly, there is a geographical pattern of housing opportunities, secondly, another pattern of housing needs, and thirdly, a pattern of local housing policies. In an ideal situation the distribution of housing needs on the one hand and of opportunities and policies on the other would match. In other words any individual in a given area with given needs would find an acceptable solution to these needs and the local authority housing policy would be operating so as to facilitate and maintain this situation. This is evidently the sort of out-come that central government has in mind when it advocates comprehensive housing policies to local authorities.

As we have seen this ideal situation is far from being realized. The major problem is that the territorial distribution of the three factors—policies, needs, and opportunities—far from matching each other often conflict. This was most apparent in the case of Lambeth and least so in the case of Sutton and, in more general terms, in the case of Inner and Outer London respectively.

Sutton was largely a middle-class area and certainly in the past the bulk of those living there could afford to find private-sector solutions. Sutton's policies, based on this assumption, were designed to marginally alter the activities of some agencies. In reality the meshing together of policies, needs, and oppor-tunities in Sutton was not quite so perfect. Even in this outer area, our work showed that a gap appeared to be growing between the desire for private-sector housing and the ability of the agencies to provide it at the right price, if at all. At the same time there was an unrecognized need for public housing in the borough.

Compared with Lambeth though, Sutton had a high degree of convergence between the three main elements, policies, needs, and opportunities. Throughout this book we have seen how the geographical distribution of housing opportunities in Lambeth failed to match the distribution of need. This was most clear in the chapters on private developers and building societies, neither of whom was able to offer any significant opportunities in Inner London. However the opportunities that were open to people in such areas through public housing and housing associations were also highly constrained. These agencies were unable to offer anywhere near a sufficient level of opportunities to meet demand. Private landlords and estate agents were equally unable or unwilling to meet the housing needs of the population. On the one hand they were opting out altogether or concentrating on the upper end of the market, on the other hand offering a declining and deteriorating stock of accom-modation to those who failed to find other solutions. It was the existence of this situation which provided the main reason for Lambeth's wholly different 'regulatory' strategy, attempting to increase both public and private-sector output. But Lambeth faced the additional problem in trying to match policies, needs, and opportunities that its policies were dependent on opportunities being provided by other *public* agencies too. Unlike Sutton, Lambeth's comprehensive approach was dependent on an increased contribution from the GLC and from outer boroughs such as Sutton. Lambeth's policy here had implications for territories other than its own which they on the whole were not prepared to accept.

This now raises the whole question of the efficiency of the comprehensive policies we have been looking at and the nature of the problems they faced.

Local Ideologies, Constraints, and Comprehensive Housing Policies

Having examined agency by agency and area by area the interplay of ideologies and constraints we can now see where the main difficulties lie in achieving the goals of the three authorities' comprehensive policies.

It is clear that there is often just as little scope for local authorities to alter the constraints affecting other agencies as there is for them to affect their ideologies. Furthermore even when they can alter constraints, however minimally, the changes effected may merely shift the problems round in a complex and interlocking system, rather than contributing to their solution. It is also clear that this complexity and interconnectedness often means that the consequences of action taken by one authority in pursuit of its version of a comprehensive policy, while achieving its own particular goals, may have unforeseen and/or adverse effects on another authority and the policy it is pursuing. Again a problem is being shifted round the system rather than being solved.

All these points have been illustrated by our work. The ruling group in Lambeth, while able and indeed finding it necessary to alter their own ideology, had as little success in altering the constraints affecting an agency as altering the ideology of that agency. Thus we saw how difficult it was to get agencies such as developers and landlords—which are private, profit-oriented organizations—and building societies—which are averse to risk taking—to operate as Lambeth wished them to. There were various reasons for this. In some cases the constraints facing the agencies were so powerful that they could not do what Lambeth required and maintain their essential profit-making requirement. In other cases the ideology of the organization was averse to such a change anyway, as in the case of the building societies. In the case of large landlords it was only when the help that Lambeth could offer happened to coincide with the goals dictated by their own ideology and constraints that meaningful co-operation was possible. However conditions in the Lambeth area were such as to make the net outcome of this co-operation of very little overall significance in meeting housing needs. Furthermore even in Sutton we suggested that when the council's policies could not overcome the constraints facing developers to the extent that the developer's ideology required, the results would be disappointing. However the most important problem created by differing ideologies which our work showed was the conflict between Lambeth's policies on the one hand and the GLC's and Sutton's on the other. Lambeth wanted them to make more public housing available but this they were not willing to do.

Sometimes more could be achieved when the organization shared the same ideology as the council and when the real problem was one of constraints. Thus Lambeth was able to obtain a high degree of co-operation from various housing associations by reducing or removing the constraints they faced. In consequence they contributed to the council's goals. The GLC and Sutton also, but in a differing way, co-operated successfully with the associations.

But in general no matter what the ideology was, two sorts of constraints were not amenable to change. The first were those imposed by the market system for housing and land and the difficulties this created for the local authorities and the housing associations, who have to compete for land and property within it. The second concerned the impact of central government policies and the policies being pursued by other housing authorities. We saw how, for example, the government's emphasis on house improvement made it harder for Lambeth (and Sutton) to secure land for redevelopment, how inadequate legislation could handicap the public health inspectorate's operations, how subsidy arrangements could affect the size of dwellings produced by housing associations, and so on. Equally the policies being pursued by other local authorities created

problems for Lambeth in particular. Thus the GLC in achieving
its aim of pumping a great deal of money into housing associations disrupted Lambeth's arrangements. Lambeth in achieving its own goal of reducing multiple occupation probably
shifted the problem to surrounding inner and outer boroughs
rather than eliminating it.

In general the high degree of interconnectedness between the
organizations working in the different local authority areas
means that a policy may have far reaching and sometimes
negative consequences. Lambeth for instance had a large
clearance programme, an extensive system controlling the
privately-rented sector and a weak mortgage scheme because
of a division of departmental responsibilities. Yet if mortgage
applications could not use the local authority as 'lender of last
resort', their demand for funds would be satisfied by other
means. Finance companies filled this gap and charged what the
market would bear. At the same time estate agents were search-
ing for a new role in Lambeth because of the loss of properties
they managed through extensive redevelopment and because of
the controls of the public health inspectorate. Agents who were
not guided by a professional code could take advantage of the
demand for house purchase. This came from people who,
because of the clearance programme priorities of the local
authority and the rapidly shrinking private-rented sector, were
unable to find another form of secure housing. The agents
formed links with the finance companies and referred potential
purchasers there. Estate agents in Outer London could act as
lending agents for building societies in the outer area. The
estate agents operating in the inner areas did not receive such
quotas, only from societies trying to compete by 'carving out' a
particular new part of the market. But because of the investor-
oriented outlook of all the societies this was still very limited.
This led mortgage applicants to the local authority, thence to
estate agents and finance companies. The process comes full
circle.

The greatest difficulties in achieving comprehensive policies
were found in Lambeth. The action it took had dramatic,
unforeseen, or uncontrollable consequences for other organizations because of the way the different agencies were dependent on one another. In general it seems that the territorial
basis of local comprehensive policies and their territorial

limitations in the metropolitan area of London, means that those boroughs facing the worst housing situation, often even if willing to use all the powers, sanctions, bargains, and controls that they can, are the least able to achieve anything. Those with more power—because the political and economic structure makes other areas dependent on them—tend to be less willing to adopt the 'appropriate' comprehensive approach. Where the territories of the powerless and the powerful overlap there is conflict, as we saw with the operations of housing associations. Where they do not overlap there is conflict again as we saw with the different attitudes that Lambeth and Sutton had to the need for more public housing. The situation is not amenable to solution via the collection of more information on gaps in service provision. The solution lies in the redistribution of power between organizations. No local authority can achieve much by itself and so it is to central government that we must now turn.

Central Government and the Organization of Housing

If change requires a redistribution of power between organizations there are two questions which need to be asked of central government. The first concerns the feasibility of government being able to act in this way, but the second more immediate question is whether government policies give any indication that this is a course which they are likely to adopt.

Furthermore different authorities have interpreted their powers and duties in different ways. The different approaches to what can be generally termed a 'comprehensive' policy demonstrates this. These differences in London have led to conflict and have contributed in large measure to the relative failure of a determined 'comprehensive' approach in the inner area. But no real account is taken by central government of the distribution of organizational power in urban areas which this situation reflects.

In this chapter we have shown how the disjunction between the territorially-defined factors of housing policies, needs, and opportunities is the source of the continuing housing problem. We have also referred to the ideal situation where these factors converge, where an individual in need in a given area could find an acceptable solution to his need and local authority policy would operate to facilitate and maintain this situation. It seems as if this simple and misleading model is the basis for government's advocacy of comprehensive policy. Together with this view, that the housing system is basically benevolent and contains within it the potential to solve all needs, go a number of linked assumptions.

Central government often refers to the fact that housing needs and conditions vary between areas but it assumes that opportunities in the housing market are stratified according to income, regardless of local variations. Thus people are assumed to be able to move from one tenure to another as their financial situation improves (or, presumably, declines). But we have seen that opportunities vary, not only according to the distribution of income, but also according to the constraints which differing geographical locations place upon organizations and people and according to the varying ideologies of the agencies on which the government's policies depend for their implementation.

Along with the assumption of a rational distribution of opportunities goes an assumption that there is an equally rational distribution of agencies, each serving different sections of the market. This is what underlies the fact that each of the agencies we have analysed is given an equal legitimacy in legislation. Help given to one set of agencies serving one market is seen as enabling it to achieve its goals without affecting other agencies serving other parts of the distribution. However as we have seen the result is often that housing policies are contradictory, in the sense that while achieving one aim they simultaneously reduce the chances of other equally valued aims being attained. It is clear that if the main aim of the 'comprehensive' approach is the relief of housing need then all existing housing agencies should not be regarded as having equal legitimacy—while continuing to play their current roles at least—because this preserves the *status quo* with regard to the relative degrees of power in the system that these agencies have. Instead a redistribution of power is required.

If the model outlined above is implicitly that held by central government then the resulting policy that emerges will be a series of piecemeal reactions to problems as they arise, with very little concern shown for the systematic implications of the new proposals, rather than a thoroughgoing reappraisal of the system and a series of policies which reflect a clear choice of priorities. Recent government policies confirm that it is the former rather than the latter approach which is being taken. An 'Action Group' has been set up to try and resolve the conflict of interests between inner and outer boroughs regarding land and housing availability. Attempts are being made to rationalize housing association activity through 'zoning' and by channelling subsidy to them through the Housing Corporation rather than the local authorities. The building societies have been offered a grant to subsidize their interest rate to borrowers and are being urged to consider a stabilization fund and differential interest rates to borrowers. Private developers are being encouraged to go into partnership with local authorities and/or to build on subsidized land. At the same time it is hoped that a land-hoarding charge will ensure the release of more land. Private landlords are now able to negotiate 'agreed' rents rather than regulated ones and their tenants are to receive rent allowances. Public housing tenants now pay 'fair' rents and the new subsidy system is intended to concentrate help on areas where it is most needed.

When many of these proposals, especially those which aim to alter the behaviour of agencies, are matched against what we have learnt from their operations, their inadequacy becomes evident. The Action Group, consisting of politicians from local and central government, has no executive powers and has been largely a means of postponing action on the difficulties of the metropolitan area rather than a part of a more 'comprehensive' approach, because in the end it must rely on co-operation between independent authorities as the present system does.[1] The 'zoning' of housing associations will still not

---

[1] In a written answer in *Hansard* on 9 August, 1972, Reginald Eyre, the Under-Secretary of State at the Department of the Environment, commented on the second report of the Action Group on land availability and requirements. He welcomed suggestions that had emerged from the Action Group's report that there were 140 acres in the docks, and 160 acres which British Rail could make available, but he underlined the need for co-operation between boroughs in helping to solve the housing shortage.

'The Group has recognized that this co-operation between the differing and at times conflicting interests concerned in London is essential if the housing shortage is to be reduced effectively. In following up the

lessen the competition from potential owner occupiers or developers, nor enable a borough like Lambeth to move more people to other boroughs. Perhaps the freedom of associations to obtain finance from the Housing Corporation rather than the local authorities will tie them less to local policies and this may mean that they can rehouse people from Inner London in Outer London. But, unless special steps are taken to bring it about, this would only arise by accident, as with local authority mortgage schemes. There is certainly nothing in central government thinking to this effect. In any case such a development would also mean that inner boroughs like Lambeth would lose what control they have on the associations in their areas. Building societies will still remain investor-oriented using a strict interpretation of security and 'status' no matter how their total lending is 'stabilized' from year to year and charging differential interest rates to borrowers will not change this. Local authority mortgage schemes which borrowers could turn to are ignored. Nothing will persuade private developers to develop land before they can get a good return on it—nor will cheaper land or higher densities ensure cheaper housing, since developers base their price on what people will pay not what the land costs or what densities are allowed. The constraints on the private landlord are eased, and house improvement unconditionally encouraged. To help private tenants pay the higher rents which result, rent allowances have been introduced. At the same time government argues that to give furnished tenants the same security as unfurnished tenants would reduce the privately-rented stock even further by imposing another

---

survey the Group will not be seeking to impose predetermined proposals on individual boroughs. There are a variety of ways and many aspects in which the borough can make a contribution to solving London's housing problems, varying from increasing the stock of publicly-owned dwellings on the one hand to promoting the construction of more houses for owner occupation, particularly in the lower price ranges, on the other—including improvement work and measures to increase the contribution made by housing societies and associations. The Group will wish to seek the co-operation of individual boroughs to establish which of the alternative activities will together enable them the best contribution without losing their own essential characteristics.'

House of Commons Debates, Written Answers, 9 August, 1972. Col. 433-7.

constraint on landlords. But the shortage of privately-rented housing is only important because councils in hard pressed areas are unable to build enough public housing in their own area and are unable to persuade the metropolitan authority to ease their land problem by rehousing sufficient people elsewhere. Increased building subsidies to areas in need do not help this because the land problem is ignored.

With every step central and local government get more and more involved in the organization of housing but the net effect and even the precise aims of this policy becomes more and more difficult to assess[2] as the territorial limitations of the system we have outlined are largely ignored.

The fact is that government is trying to impose its conception of a 'comprehensive' policy on a system of housing opportunities which has been the result of a gradual accumulation of powers, controls, and communication processes. We have shown that the organization of housing is an amalgam of directive and permissive powers controlled by various, often conflicting, processes of accountability. As a result it contains the array of overlapping and competing organizations we described earlier in this chapter. Furthermore each organization performs an important intervening role in those areas of policy whose implementation it is entrusted with. This means that it may misinterpret, neglect, or transmute legislation or policy expectations. This intervening role becomes all the more important because of the lack of one comprehensive, concerted system of housing—in fact the system could be better characterized as a 'disorganization of housing'.

Apart from the question of whether central government recognizes these complexities there is the problem of whether, given such a recognition, effective changes could be made. This must be doubtful for, as in the politics of decision-making in Lambeth, Sutton, and the GLC, social policy at central government level is the result of the interplay of different interests with different outlooks and different amounts of

---

[2] One commentator had this to say on the White Paper, *Widening the Choice: The Next Steps in Housing* (London: H.M.S.O., 1973). 'A makeshift policy, fortified now by a home inventory catalogue of good intentions, strange contraptions, and bits of string.' *The Guardian*, 10 April, 1973.

power. Policy is the result of compromise and influence where powerful pressure groups play a vital role.[3]

However when more radical alternatives begin to be expressed by powerful groups within the political system, or when new groups with the ability to exert strong pressure arise, change may occur. In the Introduction we referred to variations on the third concept of 'comprehensive' housing policy, which involved more radical intervention and the recognition of firstly, some of the territorial constraints we have outlined and secondly, the need to discriminate between agencies. In the final section we shall discuss some of the unanswered questions which this approach raises.

Towards a Need-oriented Housing Policy

Lambeth's changing policies illustrate the situation where existing or new groups within the political system have committed themselves to a need-oriented approach and begin to propose new ways of meeting these when present policies fail. Having obtained the maximum degree of co-operation they could from the GLC and the outer boroughs within the existing system and having come up against the difficulties we have outlined, they, together with other Inner London boroughs, were largely instrumental in setting up the Action Group and the London Boroughs' Association's London Housing Office.[4] Other inner boroughs have taken even more

---

[3] For example, see Barnett, M. J. *The Politics of Legislation* (London: Weidenfeld and Nicolson, 1969).

[4] The London Housing Office was set up in 1972 along with the Action Group. The London Housing Office was to produce up-to-date statistics on housing needs and resources, assess the help which outer boroughs might give to inner areas, and to organize the movement of people from Inner to Outer London.

Only twenty-two of the thirty-two London boroughs (including the City of London) agreed to participate; those which declined were, (a) Inner London: Kensington and Chelsea, Southwark, and (b) Outer London: Barnet, Bromley, Croydon, Enfield, Hounslow, Kingston, Redbridge, Richmond, and Sutton.

Sutton thought that another body concerned with London housing was unnecessary. The Leader of the Council was already a member of the Action Group although there is presumably supposed to be some link between the Group and the London Boroughs' London Housing Office.

direct action by trying to build on land in Outer London.[5] The London Labour Party has proposed the abolition of the privately-rented landlord in their plan to municipalize rented property over a ten-year period [1]. The Layfield Report on the Greater London Development Plan has suggested that the GLC might be relieved of its role as London's strategic housing authority [2].

Behind this newly emergent set of proposals there can be seen a shift towards the more radical end of the third sort of 'comprehensive' policy we have described, at least in so far as these proposals reject the view that the public and private sectors can with marginal adjustments exist side by side or that there are identities of interest between different parts of the public sector. But as yet the proponents of these new policies are following the familiar piecemeal approach and failing to appreciate the impact and implications of their proposals for the whole housing system. Those who propose these new policies have to be capable of answering a whole series of questions if their suggestions are not merely to impose still further complexities and uncertainties on an already complex and uncertain system and if they are to achieve their goal of a more need-oriented housing system.

Taking the strategic housing authority first, how would a particular (presumably progressive) ideology be assured, one that would intervene where necessary and redistribute access to land? Who would appoint it or elect it, what would be its electoral constituency, to whom then would it be accountable? Is it to be involved with public housing only, in which case is it to stop private development to ensure adequate public provision, and if so, how? Is owner occupation to be stopped from increasing, especially in Inner London? If it is not concerned solely with public housing what power would it have to bargain with private enterprise which, as we have seen, has a particular set of constraints and accountabilities to reckon with? How is it to handle the network of interlocking, inter-dependent

---

[5] Croydon has refused an application by Lambeth for permission to build 1500 dwellings on land owned by Lambeth in Croydon. Barnet refused to accept a bid for a housing site from Brent despite it being the highest made. Barnet agreed to sell to a private developer instead. London Council of Social Service, *London's Housing Needs* (London: LCSS, 1973).

organizations we described earlier? Where would it get its money from, and how much? What powers would it have to redistribute people and the use of space? What would be its relationship with the GLC and how would it fit into more general planning policy for which the GLC has metropolitan responsibility?[6]

Some of these questions also apply to the strategy which aims at municipalizing the privately-rented stock, particularly the question of the wider planning issues. But in addition to this, the question which emerges from our research is what is to happen to the tenants of property who have a resident landlord. These properties would be defined as 'owner-occupied' according to the municipalization argument. But according to our research it was just these properties where the greatest amount of stress occurred. Here the landlord needed the tenants to help him pay off an extortionate mortgage. But the stresses and strains of landlord/tenant relationships in these circumstances produced the greatest threat to the security of tenure for the tenants. So if security of tenure is to be achieved through municipalizing the rented stock then what about the owner occupied properties where this security is weakest? Furthermore so far as this type of owner-occupied property is concerned, what can the municipalization strategy do about the ability of wealthy people to acquire more housing space by virtue of their superior purchasing power? Are rich people to be allowed to buy out resident landlords when these landlords

---

[6] This last point is particularly important because both Lambeth and the GLC aimed at maintaining particular population and employment levels which were seen as essential to the economic base of their particular area but which would conflict with the decline of population implied by a comprehensive housing strategy such as Lambeth's. This raises questions about conflicting ideologies and organizations in planning which is a topic of study in its own right. We mentioned the conflict in Lambeth in Chapter One. All we can add here is that the whole field of planning should be looked at in the same way that we have considered the organization of housing. Questions should be asked as to whether 'comprehensive' or strategic housing policies, for instance, should include employment needs when housing need is assessed since people need to be able to match their housing and employment opportunities far more closely than at present. If employment is to be stimulated or controlled by planners in different areas then what of people's associated housing needs and demands?

find they cannot continue with the extortionate mortgage repayments, and thereby replace three or four poor families with one rich one? In other words, what is the full extent of the municipalization policy, what are the controls over private enterprise, and how are they to be implemented?

Finally, if some of the increasingly publicly-owned stock is to be handed over to housing associations, to diversify ownership, how are they to fit into the overall picture? Are they to be allowed to close waiting lists when they choose, and are they to use their own sometimes arbitrary criteria for selecting tenants? How are their ideologies and constraints to be overcome and incorporated in an overall strategy?

In other words, 'radical alternatives' to aspects of the present organization of housing raise more questions than they answer. However the purpose of this study is not to suggest alternative policies. It is to demonstrate that, *whatever* new housing policy is proposed, those who put it forward and those who operate existing policies would be better equipped at least to understand the impact of these policies if they were aware of the significance of ideologies, constraints, and the resultant interaction and dependencies of agencies. So far as a more need-oriented housing policy is concerned, radical political changes would be required to achieve this goal, as our study has shown that the present housing system—which is far from meeting this goal—is hinged on the distribution of power at central government and city level.

References

1. Labour Party Manifesto. *A Socialist Strategy for London.* GLC Election, London, 1973.
2. GLDP. *Written Statement* (London: GLC, 1969).

Appendix

Methodology

Reasons are given in the Introduction for the choice of Lambeth and Sutton as the main geographical areas in which to conduct the research. These two areas were archetypical of the polarization of housing conditions in London as a whole, the one being an area of stress and the other showing very little stress. Also, being in the same geographic sector of London, it seemed likely that if Lambeth had to look beyond its borders for help it would be to areas such as Sutton, rather than for example a North-West outer area.

In addition both Lambeth, Sutton, and the GLC too, had a 'comprehensive' approach to housing but with rather different emphasis. Of course not all housing organizations have a specific territorial base and in these cases the information that the research obtained about their general operations had then to be applied to the specific areas we were concerned with. Sometimes, as in the chapters on building societies and private developers, we found that some of the agencies we interviewed were playing no role at all in one or both of our main study areas. However it was still necessary to study their operations as they were seen rightly or wrongly by the various advocates of a 'comprehensive' housing policy as having a role to play in their areas. Hence the necessity to see whether this expectation could hope to be fulfilled by understanding where, how and why these agencies were operating.

Certain problems arose in the selection of agencies. The idea of a 'representative' sample of a given category of agencies according to criteria of number of dwellings, resources or whatever only has limited validity in a study which is not primarily concerned to investigate the operations of agencies in a given category as an end in itself but in the context of the contribution that they were making or were asked to make to comprehensive housing policies.

Housing Associations

We chose the London and the Metropolitan Housing Trust because they were both 'general need' associations of the type Lambeth Council were trying to co-operate with. Both had sizeable and well established operations in the borough unlike most of the other associations there at the time of our research and would therefore be looked to in any comprehensive policy of the Lambeth type. In fact both had been given special help by the borough. The Family Housing Association qualified as a GLC-backed association on the same grounds although in retrospect it would have been useful to have looked at a GLC-backed association whose operations were less socially oriented. The Sutton associations were chosen on similar criteria.

Building Societies

We chose two large national societies which on the face of it, could be expected to do a good deal of business in our areas and also one regional society which operated particularly in South London and the southern Home Counties and, in addition, had a reputation for being prepared to lend on the older property characteristic of an inner area such as Lambeth. Finally we tried to find a small local society to see whether they were more likely to be able to operate in areas disliked by the larger concerns. We could only find one, based on Lambeth, and as it turned out it was more rather than less conservative regarding where and how it would lend.

Private Landlords and Estate Agents

We explained in the text our concentration on the larger landlords, plus agents as representatives of smaller landlords and as agencies operating in the rented market in their own right, and in addition two of the 'establishment' landlords—the latter being selected because they had significant holdings in Lambeth.

As far as the selection of agents and company landlords was concerned we obtained a rough distribution of the numbers of properties owned and managed by these agencies in Lambeth and Sutton by an analysis of the rating lists for the two boroughs. From this and other sources, especially Rent Officer and Tribunal Records and Lambeth's register of multi-occupation, we selected a range of landlords and agents which seemed fairly representative of the totality of these agencies operating in the two areas and which would have to be involved in 'comprehensive' policies.

Private Developers

Here we tried to obtain a representative selection of builders. At a rough estimate between 80–90 per cent of builders in Great Britain start twenty or less houses per year. However the proportion of the total number of privately-built houses which they built amounted to only 25 per cent in 1969 and 30 per cent in 1970. Although perhaps only 1 per cent of builders start more than 150 houses a year, they nevertheless built over 40 per cent of the houses started in 1969 and 1970. For our study, 'large' builders were defined as those building 500 or more per annum, and 'medium' builders, those starting 400 or thereabout and less. This is because one large builder felt that 300–400 per year was the make-or-break point for expansion into the big league, particularly in overcoming land constraints, and we found that this appeared to be true. Those firms building between 200 and 400 per annum experienced problems which definitely distinguished them from the vast concerns of the big builders but they were nevertheless of a completely different nature from the small firms that we chose. The range of 'smallness' may well stretch up to 100 or slightly more but in London we believe that the constraints confine small firms to far less and that this quite suits the goals of these firms, as we explain in Chapter Six. We chose to study two small builders (less than twenty houses started per annum) and two medium builders (less than 400 per annum). All these were concentrated in Sutton. We also looked at three large builders (over 1000 per annum) who were not necessarily working in either of our two boroughs but, as it happened, two of them had built in Sutton in the past.

Much of the sociological literature on organizations has been concerned with the internal dynamics of organizations. Taking the goals as given, studies have shown how these are transmitted through the organization, modified, or transmuted. We were more concerned to identify the goals and ideologies of the organizations and see how they could be related to a coherent housing policy incorporating the attitudes and operations of these organizations. We were concerned with the organization in its socio-economic environment, for it is necessary to study the way in which an organization interacts with its environment in order to understand the content of its ideology and goals, the problems of resource procurement, and most of the major constraints (including the operations of other, especially housing, agencies) which together determine the characteristic pattern of action of an organization. Of course this is not to say that some purely internal factors do not affect this pattern. An example would be the educational processes through which building society staff go, and the internal conflict between the goal of the Housing Directorate and the operations of the Finance Directorate in the implementation of Lambeth's mortgage scheme. However our analysis of the organizations' operations was sufficiently wide ranging to reveal most of these major internal factors while concentrating on the broad general features of the organization and its environment.

The second major area of work concerned itself with attempting to gain an understanding of the types of housing need which the agencies were meeting or helping to meet. Of course some indication of this was gained from our interviews with the agencies but wherever possible a fuller and more accurate picture was obtained by statistical analysis of samples of the agencies' own client records. The quality and amount of data varied and in one or two cases the agency only gave us a limited period in which to do the work but the general aim was to collect demographic and socio-economic details along with information about previous and present housing conditions. A large number of tabulations were prepared many of which confirmed the picture we had gained of the people the agencies served from our studies of their operations. In consequence we have made as sparing a use as possible of these data in the text in order to avoid much tedious repetition. For similar reasons we have also assumed a fair level of understanding of housing

practice and legislation and the current London housing
situation. Wherever appropriate, references have been given to
enable those who are not familiar with these aspects to follow
them up.

Certain samples were taken outside the main agencies in
order to gain an understanding of the structure and operations
of the agencies themselves, e.g. especially the Rent Officer and
Tribunal samples used in Chapter Five. Also some of our
samples of the clients' records threw light on specific features of
the agencies' operations, e.g. the way in which the rules relating
to security and status operated in the local authority mortgage
schemes.

The main methods of work can be set out as follows:

A Appraisal of the overall housing situation and trends in the
study areas, based on an investigation of the population structure, social composition, housing conditions, and income and
expenditure patterns. A variety of published and unpublished
data was used.

B Studies of the operations of the agencies, learning about their
ideologies and goals, the roles they perform and the legal,
organizational, political, and resource constraints they faced
as a result of inter- and intra-organizational factors. Interviews
with key personnel based on semi-structured questionnaires,
examination of internal documents and press coverage, and
some survey material were the main sources for this work.
Interviews took place between August 1970 and November
1971.

C Appraisal of the output of the agencies as explained above.
Brief details of the various sample surveys are given below:

1 Five samples of local authority tenants were taken:

 (a) and (b) A 1 in 6 sample of families housed by Lambeth
 and Sutton from 1965 to 1971. In the Lambeth sample
 we included tenant transfers, for reasons which we explain
 in Table 1.1 (page 27) and took a separate 1 in 6 sample
 of 'special cases' since they were comparatively few, and
 still important. In Lambeth twenty-four families were
 untraceable. We have kept the transfers separate. In
 Sutton twenty-eight of the sample were caretakers,
 other staff, temporary lettings, or untraceable. These

have all been omitted from the tabulations. Lambeth: $N = 674$, Sutton: $N = 273$.

(c) Data on nominations by Lambeth to the GLC was only kept for the previous two years by the borough. We took a 1 in 6 sample of Lambeth nominations from 1970 to 1971. None were untraceable. $N = 142$.

(d) We selected five of the twenty-one sites cleared by the GLC over the period 1965–71 in Southern District Office area. These sites together represented the three types of activity undertaken by the GLC—Part III clearance, Part V clearance, and clearance for schools and roads—in the correct proportion. This represented a 1 in 4 sample of households displaced over the period. Ten households were untraceable because they had housed themselves privately. Another thirty were untraceable when tenants were rehoused to another district or eventually to another borough. $N = 167$.

(e) Data on lettings in the St Helier District Office in the Sutton area was only available for the post-1968 period. We took a 1 in 6 sample of new lettings on GLC estates in Sutton (excluding transfers). Fifteen of the sample were untraceable. $N = 121$.

We had to limit the areas in which we would collect data for families rehoused by the GLC to the administrative areas of the two boroughs since, as with one or two other agencies, it was difficult or overly time consuming to do otherwise. A London borough is usually not part of a GLC 'district'—the administrative areas used by the GLC Housing Department. This means that we only have data on families who lived in parts of the districts which included the boroughs—Southern District of Lambeth and St Helier District for Sutton.

The boundaries of Lambeth and the Southern District are nearly coterminous. Until 1 April, 1971, the Southern District Office (SDO) managed 29 448 properties, 19 000 of which were in Lambeth, and all the rest, except one estate in Westminster, were in Southwark or Wandsworth. On 1 April 6000 dwellings were handed over to Lambeth and 2000 to Wandsworth (Southwark refused to take any). Since then the SDO has had 23 065 properties.

All of Sutton is in St Helier District. Until 1 April, 1971, the large St Helier estate in St Helier District comprised 11 360 properties. Two thousand dwellings were handed over to Sutton and Merton. There are now 5586 houses in Sutton on the estate and the remaining 3774 are in Merton. There are also 608 GLC dwellings in Sutton at Roundshaw.

There were difficulties in obtaining complete figures on previous tenure in the Lambeth tenant sample as 37 per cent of tenants were recorded as already being Lambeth tenants when rehoused. In these cases the local authority had compulsorily acquired the dwellings and the tenure prior to the acquisition was not recorded. This hardly affected waiting list cases, but for clearance cases 57 per cent were recorded as already being local authority tenants without any mention of previous tenure.

Also the samples were taken over different time spans, but there were enough households in the Lambeth and Sutton tenant samples rehoused in 1970–71 to provide income figures which could be compared to those of the Lambeth nominees for Table 1.4. Unfortunately this was not the case for other samples.

2 Three samples were taken of local authority mortgages:

(a) Sutton—A 1 in 5 sample dating from April 1965 to April 1971. $N = 221$.
(b) Lambeth—A 1 in 4 sample, dating from April 1965 to April 1971. $N = 174$.
(c) GLC—A 1 in 10 sample, dating from April 1965 to April 1971. $N = 461$.

In Lambeth and Sutton details of the previous tenure of the sample were not available.

3 We took five samples of housing association tenants in the respective boroughs:

(a) London Housing Trust—A 1 in 2 sample of all housed since it began operations in 1968. $N = 85$.
(b) Metropolitan Housing Trust—A census of existing tenants. $N = 32$.
(c) Castlemead Housing Association—Information was inadequate and a full sample impossible. Information on tenants in their old peoples' scheme only available; a census was taken. $N = 38$.

(*d*) Sutton Housing Society—A 1 in 2 sample of all lettings since they began in 1967. $N = 40$.

(*e*) Family Housing Association—A 1 in 2 sample of all lettings since FHA commenced operation in Lambeth. Information was lacking on nine households. $N = 85$.

It can be seen that these samples were inadequate in a number of respects.

4 The Department of the Environment made available special tabulations of their 1970 5 per cent sample building society survey. This is a stratified sample which reflects the predominance of the larger societies in the total pattern of lending.

For the sample of all building societies for Group A boroughs, $N = 325$, for Group B, $N = 1539$. Most reliance was placed in the text on these two samples but in addition samples were available for all building societies by Lambeth ($N = 25$) and Sutton ($N = 55$). Also we had samples for our four selected societies by Groups A and B boroughs and by Lambeth and Sutton respectively. In these latter cases most of the samples were too small for reliance to be placed on them but some apparent corroboration of the evidence from the larger samples was possible.

5 One landlord enabled us to sample client records. Because of the inadequate number of properties the firm had in Sutton we took a sample of properties in Lambeth and Sutton plus the neighbouring outer borough of Bromley. The sample was of those who had become tenants in 1970–71. After deducting properties which had been resold from the sample of relets we ended up with forty-four in Lambeth and twenty-seven from Sutton/Bromley. Unfortunately this is only a 1 in 10 sample.

6 Four samples of the Rent Officers' and Rent Tribunals' cases in Lambeth and Sutton were taken.

(*a*) Rent Officers in Lambeth—A 1 in 5 sample of all applications from their inception in 1965 until 1971. $N = 805$.

(*b*) Rent Officers in Sutton—A 1 in 3 sample, other details as above. $N = 442$.

(c) Lambeth Rent Tribunal—A 1 in 5 sample of all applications from 1969 to 1971. $N = 830$.

(d) Sutton Rent Tribunal—A census (as numbers were small) from 1965 to 1971. $N = 110$.

We were concerned with data on those actually housed or given mortgages by the agencies concerned, not those who did not get housed, i.e. unsuccessful applicants—so that in this respect data from the agencies' own records was more adequate than it would have been had the focus of our study been different (i.e. on those who lose out).

Index

TOWN DEVELOPMENT ACT 1952,
   and GLC, 26

WAITING LIST, rehousing from, in
   Lambeth, 37, 38

in Sutton, 38
Walker, Peter, Secretary of
   State for the Environment,
   and financial allocation for
   private land assembly, 134